EXPERIENCING GOD
Thoughts and Testimonies

Robin Arthur

Foreword by Ivan Arthur
Author of *Pavement Prayers* and the *Fourteen Stations,* Official Souvenir of Pope John Paul II's visit to India

En Route Books and Media, LLC
5705 Rhodes Avenue
St. Louis, MO 63109

⊕ *ENROUTE*
Make the time

Cover design: Aaron Arthur. Image: Sahara Prince via Shutterstock. The cover depicts the biblical narrative of the burning bush at Mount Sinai from where God spoke to Moses and appointed him to lead the Israelites out of Egypt and into Canaan.

ISBN-13: 978-1-952464-89-8
Library of Congress Control Number: 2021940537
Copyright © 2021 Robin Arthur

To my father, Jossie
(1913-1978)

A man of God and a guiding light to the family

CONTENTS

FOREWORD

"Never discuss politics or religion - that is, if you want to keep your friends," my father had said to me at a time when the fur over my lips and the brashness of that age called for the razor. Looking back, I have lost arguments and sometimes my voice in those many high decibel, table thumping parlour crusades we fought in our youth, but I cannot remember having lost a friend. Those early jousts were refereed by (priests from the Archdiocese of Bombay) Fr. Vincent Alvares and Fr. Siolkar, between and among an all-Catholic group of sodalists when pages torn from the *Catechism of the Catholic Church* joined and sometimes crossed swords with Fulton Sheen, C.S. Lewis, Thomas Merton, Karl Rahner and Hans Küng. Good religious jousting it was in which an embarrassing church history, dogma, bigotry, ritual and reform were tackled in those tournaments of juvenile theology.

Later, I remember my discussions with non-Catholics – Protestant, Hindu and Muslim – as something else: illuminating, mind-opening sessions in which faith for us began to embrace a much larger divinity that stretched from the personal to the universal dimension, breaking the fetters of a catechism that chained it to the pews of a church.

So, dad, I have news for you. You can talk about God and still keep your friends.

That is what Robin Arthur has done in his two books, the earlier *Science and the God Elusion* and now the one you have in your hand: *Experiencing God – Thoughts and Testimonies*. In doing so, I dare say he has, in fact, enlarged his circle of friends, belying my dear father's cautionary advice. He has won friends and influenced people with his writing, and for a good reason, I would say. The believers and the non-believers among his readers have both been given plenty of intellectual stimulation to excite them into either exuberant acquiescence or stout challenge. In his book *Science and the God Elusion*, the title of which pays a not-so-sly reverse tribute to the book by the world's most famous atheist of the day, Arthur points an array of artillery against a scientific mind-set that negates the existence of God and the idea that Science and Religion are irreconcilable enemies of each other.

With scholarly ammunition borrowed from Western and Oriental philosophies and religions, not shying away from the agnostics and atheists, Arthur demonstrates that science and religion do not cancel out each other. When it comes to proving the existence of God, however, science does not possess the eyes to see or for that matter recognise God even if He were to shake hands with it. Divinity is not found at the end of a theorem, or a syllogism or under the world's most powerful lenses. God has to be seen through the eyes of faith.

This came home to him even more strongly in a real and compelling way during the many online seminars in which his readers discussed the book, voiced their approval and challenged some of his ideas. It strengthened his conviction that 'all the king's horses and all the king's men' in study and argument, may at a push, engender a slender belief that a God exists but that no amount of reason or scholarly bombarding can engender faith. You do not just believe in God; you have to experience God.

So this book, *Experiencing God,* had to be written.

Arthur had once said that his belief in God was not a blind one: it was based on reason; an assertion that he later thought fit to edit, quietly shifting that 'belief' into the realm of faith, citing the famous Thomasine Finger-in-His-side as best describing his personal God experience. In *Experiencing God*, Arthur uses the same learned ammunition from *Science and the God Elusion,* and some more, to describe the various manifestations of that Finger-in-His-side; that moment when doubt bypasses belief, the offspring of reason, to step into the luminescent circle of the spirit and of faith. From here, you may see God as in Moses' burning bush or hear that still, small voice in Elijah's ear.

Arthur clearly delineates the boundaries of belief and faith with insights from mystics such as Thomas Merton and others, including bold interjections from popular science as in the podcasts of Mike McHargue who presents proof that religion and spirituality are as much at home in the convolutions of the brain as our thoughts and feelings. Intuitively, we may agree and yet dig deep down into our beings in an earnest desire to mine that precious nugget we know as faith.

It is all very well, Robin Arthur, you might say, to talk about faith as experienced by mystics like Merton or Teresa of Avila or John of the Cross or the Sufi saints. Where is that Finger-in-His-Side for simple but ardent searchers of the Experience like me and my cousin? The yogi offers me transcendental meditation, the Sufi shows me the whirling dance of the dervish and the Catholic priest will administer the sacraments right up to my last breath. We have heard of the miracles at Lourdes and Fatima, or even closer home from friends and relatives who say that they experienced God after having been miraculously healed at the Potta shrine in the Indian state of Kerala, or at the parish charismatic prayer meeting. And we thrash and flounder in our search, not having to date seen a miracle, or had that life-changing experience.

Experiencing God hints at channels of grace and faith; other 'sacraments' (if one may call them that) that may lead one to the burning bush. In pointing to prayer, suffering, tribulation and even martyrdom as portals to that Experience, Arthur joins a learned chorus of mystics, saints and theologians, Christian and non-Christian, who give witness to the workings of this spiritual gift, the implicit trust in a God we cannot see.

Cutting through catechetics, pious instruction and the teachings of the world's spiritual leaders, I see the abovementioned channels of faith flowing out of one source: *The Beatitudes*. Blessed are the poor in spirit, the humble, the meek, the merciful, the suffering, the persecuted. For theirs is the kingdom of heaven, a heaven of closeness to God.

The book holds out the promise that faith in God and the experience that unlocks it can then 'happen' to anyone open to it. It does so in presenting the experiences of well-known mystics and a few simple people for whom a single episode was enough to change their lives. From the extraordinary encounter of Paul on his road to Damascus to conversion testimonies of scientists and thinkers including Francis Collins, C.S. Lewis, Joseph Pearce, Kevin Vost and his own close family members, Robin translates the theology of Faith into the probability of everybody's everyday life.

I see *Experiencing God* following an inevitable path of Robin Arthur's intellectual journey. As a journalist who teased world events into personal opinion, shaped irrepressibly by a moral bias of which he may not have been conscious, he was driven very early in his writing career to publish his first book *Can the Poor Inherit the Earth?* in which he sought to stir the conscience of world governments and social agencies to relook at the dynamics of progress in their villages.

In time, it would prompt him to envision a forum for interfaith discussion and dialogue. Thus, he instituted what many consider a cultural breakthrough in Halifax – the Spiritual Diversity Conferences. He has, to date, led three of them at which he invited internationally renowned religious leaders and theologians from all faiths to speak and exchange ideas.

With the pandemic calling a halt to subsequent conferences, Arthur decided to replicate those conventions within the covers of his two books. Citadels of faith, constructed with the help of scholarly scaffolding and personal insight, both *Science and the God Elusion* and *Experiencing God* offer believers and atheists an intellectual handle on the one hand and challenge on the other for whichever side they are on.

Faith as seen in people we know is like a beautiful garment we would like to own and wear but don't know where to buy it from. Maybe, just maybe, *Experiencing God* could direct you to that Faith Store, that Upper Room where you might be able to put your finger in His side and say, "My Lord and my God."

Ivan Arthur

INTRODUCTION

Since the Covid-19 pandemic broke out in China, we speak increasingly of dark times that have, like a cloud cover, engulfed us, and it reminds me of the song *The Sound of Silence* by the American duo Simon and Garfunkel. The author Paul appears to paint darkness as existential angst and defines silence as a cancer that grows. He speaks of neon lights that split the night, of people talking without speaking, hearing without listening, writing songs that voices never share.

Now, consider a leap from the song's analogy of a chaotic world to the godless one we see ourselves in. Why do I sympathize with the atheist? I do that because I think that someone who does not care about where man has come from, why man is here and where man is going from hereon, is a wanderer in the wilderness, floating around without a sense of purpose, a man lost on an island like the proverbial Rip van Winkle. Now this is a man who must be awakened.

This book is a sequel to *Science and the God Elusion* which I released in July 2019. It presented compelling arguments about the mysteries of the universe that have baffled scientists to this day. It affirms that the Big Bang cries out for a divine explanation and that the hypothesis presented on the origins of life on earth is ridden with serendipity. The book seeks to bring together all of these scientific and theological conversations to one table so as to open a new window and insight into the God that eludes scientific investigation and presents its wonder through mystical realms.

Experiencing God: Thoughts and Testimonies presents my perspectives on what the God experience is about through two sections of this book. In the first, I seek an understanding of Mysticism, Faith and Prayer, Suffering and Death and the Purpose of Life: Where do we come from and where are we going?

The chapter on Mysticism narrates a couple of mystical experiences told by people such as Thomas Merton – the great Trappist Monk of the Abbey of Gethsemani, Kentucky, in the 1950s, who encountered his dead father in a one-on-one, in his room in the night with the lights on. I present a testimony also from Mike McHargue, a science expert and novelist, whose early morning visions of God on the rolling billows of the sea is a compelling narrative.

I address the conundrum of faith: When Jesus cured the leper, the blind man, the bleeding woman, He sent them away saying: Go, thy faith has healed you.

Pilgrims around the world have been witness to healing at Fatima in Portugal and Lourdes in France, shrines where you see crutches hanging in the grotto, mute witnesses to those who came crippled and left whole.

Suffering and death and the purpose of life have been conundrums, too, that have baffled great thinkers of our time and yet, the gospels of Jesus shine a light on those complex realities.

Paul, who was struck down on the road to Damascus on a mission to persecute Christians, reveals in his letters how the resurrection of Jesus Christ became the key to his making sense of his suffering. In his first letter to the Corinthians (1 Corinthians 15:14-16, NAB), he says: "And if Christ has not been raised, then empty [too] is our preaching; empty, too, your faith. Then we are also false witnesses to God, because we testified against God that he raised Christ, whom he did not raise if in fact the dead are not raised. For if the dead are not raised, neither has Christ been raised."

Of course, the book also carries an addendum with vantage viewpoints that address Sin, Free Will and Predestination and the Resurrection of Jesus. Sin, Free Will and Predestination are complex discussions but are central to the Christian understanding of the problem of evil. The Resurrection of Jesus, on the other hand, is the cornerstone of the Christian gospel, reconciling the contrite sinner with God and opening the gates of heaven to mankind for eternity.

The final chapter explores the experience of God in the midst of a pandemic that appears to have put the world on its head and got us all to sit up and think. Are there answers to the questions that have stirred up within us, as Covid-19 swept across the globe and swallowed up some 2.70 million people? Is the pandemic God's way of testing his people? This passage from scripture, reproduced below, might cast a light on that question.

In Luke (13:1-5 NAB) we read: "At that time some people who were present there told him about the Galileans whose blood Pilate had mingled with the blood of their sacrifices. He said to them in reply, "Do you think that because these Galileans suffered in this way they were greater sinners than all other Galileans? By no means! But I tell you, if you do not repent, you will all perish as they did! Or those eighteen people who were killed when the tower at Siloam fell on them—do you think they were more guilty than everyone else who lived in Jerusalem? By no means! But I tell you, if you do not repent, you will all perish as they did!"

The passages confirm that God is not the author of evil. But the call to repent and be saved is the blessed assurance. He responds with gracious compassion.

Section Two of this book, however, presents testimonies of famous men and women across the world and other people - spiritually driven individuals who have either felt the healing or saving hand of God in a near-death experience - or in other ways - and have reported a sense of having made either a conversation or a connection with Him. Their testimonies tell about a change of life, through a mystical experience, through suffering and death, a new awakening brought about by an abiding faith or through the rigorous search for the purpose of life.

Among them is John Newton (1725-1807) the slaver turned preacher, who as Master of a slave ship had mounted guns and muskets on the desk aimed at the slaves' quarters and whose slaves were lashed and put in thumbscrews to keep them quiet.

The Oxford professor, C.S. Lewis's conversion to Christianity, is another testimony. A former hard-core atheist, his books including *Mere Christianity* have brought atheists such as the world's top scientist, Dr. Francis Collins, to Jesus Christ.

Dr. Collins, who is author of *The Language of God,* also testifies in this book and narrates his journey from the thorny paths of atheism to the sacred temple of

Christ, which finally saw him one summer morning in the dewy grass of the Cascade mountains in the north-west on his knees, saying to the Lord: "I get it. I am yours. I want to be your follower from now until eternity."

Joseph Pearce, a former white supremacist, also presents a chilling story of a bitter past when he found himself groping in the unlit tunnel of racial hatred and was twice convicted under the Racial Relations Act of the United Kingdom which finally brought him to Christ while in prison.

Several other testimonies in this book will prick the ear and rivet your attention to the most profound questions that have rattled mankind and present a perspective that should, with blessed grace, bring comfort and hope to restless hearts.

SECTION 1

Experiencing God

CHAPTER 1

MYSTICISM: WHAT IS IT?

Thomas Merton, the great Trappist Monk of the Abbey of Gethsemani, Kentucky in the 1950s, who reintroduced Christians to contemplative prayer which lay dormant since the sixteenth century, narrates the pain that followed on the heels of his father's death in his influential book *Seven Storey Mountain*. The instinct to pray, he says, can come to even an atheist and while that may not prove the existence of God, at least, it demonstrates the fact that the need to worship Him is driven by our dependent natures. Then he speaks of a life-changing moment, one night in a room with the lights on:

"Suddenly it seemed to me that Father, who had now been dead more than a year, was there with me. The sense of his presence was as vivid and as real and as startling as if he had touched my arm or spoken to me. The whole thing passed in a flash, but in that flash, instantly, I was overwhelmed with a sudden and profound insight into the mystery and corruption of my own soul..."[1]

Merton says he was filled with sorrow with what he saw and that the experience brought him to prayer and to a God he had never known "to free him of the thousand terrible things that held him in their slavery."

Mike McHargue, famously known as Science Mike, likewise shares a mystical moment in his book *Finding God in the Waves* when he narrates events leading up to his departure from Christianity and then reveals how he was able to come back to it through science.

"As I stood on the beach in the wee hours of the morning, everything in my surroundings took on that stretched, translucent quality. I could see what I can only call the glory of God on the other side. I felt God with me, in me, and through me. I felt connected with the Source of Life and the Source of All. After it was over, I understood why someone would feel compelled to write about a bush that burned but was not consumed. Or a blinding light on the road to Damascus. Or an angel telling a 14-year-old virgin girl she was pregnant with the Son of God."[2]

So, what really is Mysticism?

I told Isaac - my sister Belinda's husband - in a conversation not long ago: "My faith is founded on reason."

"How do you mean?" he quipped: "Are you saying that like the apostle Thomas, you shall believe only when you have put your hand in His side?"

Isaac was referencing the gospel story of the apostle who refused to believe Jesus Christ had risen from the tomb, days after his crucifixion, and had met with his fellow disciples in the Upper Room in the Old City of Jerusalem. "Until I put my hand in His side, I shall not believe," the apostle Thomas had said.

So, in the flash of a moment, I realized my utterance lacked clarity. Of course, I would like to think that my belief is founded on reason. But faith is something else. So, I quickly responded: "No. That's not it. If that is what I meant, I would be talking 'science.' But what I am really saying is that my faith is founded on the fact that the Christ has put His hand in my side and which is why I believe. Now that's mysticism."

Kurt Vonnegut, an agnostic and one of America's great writers, says this in his book *A Man Without a Country:* "If I should ever die, God forbid, let this be my epitaph: 'The only proof he needed for the existence of God was music.'"[3] So you see, mysticism is ineffable, as the 19th-century scientist and mystic William James had observed.

The mystical experience is about connecting with the God you cannot see. It's about connecting with the mysterious. Mysticism may relate to any kind of ecstasy or altered state of consciousness.

According to Gerald James Larson, "mystical experience is an intuitive understanding and realization of the meaning of existence."[4] James McClenon notes that mysticism refers to "the doctrine that special mental states or events allow an understanding of ultimate truths."[5] According to James R. Horne, mystical illumination is "a central visionary experience that results in the resolution of a personal or religious problem.[6] But other authors point out that mysticism involves more than "mystical experience." According to Jerome Gellmann, the ultimate goal of mysticism is human transformation, not just experiencing mystical or visionary states.[7]

In an Old Testament passage (Exodus 33:17-20 NAB), God says to Moses, "This request, too, which you have made, I will carry out, because you have found favor with me and you are my intimate friend. Then Moses said, 'Please let me see your glory!' The LORD answered: I will make all my goodness pass before you, and I will proclaim my name, 'LORD,' before you; I who show favor to whom I will, I who grant mercy to whom I will. But you cannot see my face, for no one can see me and live."

That, you see, is the problem that science has with affirming or denying the existence of God. Why is that so? The short answer is that God is not a scientific question. He's a theological and philosophical subject. He is the spirit of truth and exists in the soul of his creation. He is implanted in the hearts of mankind, who sees not His face, but sees Him in the wonders of creation. So, they bow and adore Him.

Some of the testimonies that are narrated in this book speak of a mystical experience just before a conversion to faith, a direct connect with God in ways that affirm that the experience is ineffable.

John Cornwell, in his riposte to Richard Dawkins' book *The God Delusion,* writes: "At the outset of your book, you insist that religion must be scientifically or empirically verifiable. And yet for most of those who have studied religion down the ages, it is as much a product of the imagination as art, poetry and music."[8]

In one of his notes to me that outlined his view of the mystical, Reverend Father Owen Connolly, a priest who serves at the Archdiocese of Halifax in Canada, referred to an ancient mystical tradition in many of the faiths including Christianity that suggests that we are given three eyes with which to look at life. First, we have the eye of the flesh serving input such as sight; second, the eye of reason and reflection; third, the eye of mystical gaze which builds on the first two eyes, namely the eye of the heart.

Then, with a reference to Merton, Connolly talked of how mystical prayer can lead man to look at life in these dangerous times from the eye of the heart.

Merton, who wrote prolifically on spirituality and social justice, was recognized as one of those rare Western minds that opened up to the Zen experience. In his work, he discusses diverse religious concepts - early monasticism, Russian Orthodox spirituality, the Shakers, and Zen Buddhism – and makes the point that all these studies are driven by the search to grasp life's meaning through a metaphysical awareness.

Fr. Karl Rahner, a German Jesuit and one of the most influential theologians in the twentieth century, said sometime before his death: "The only Christians who will survive in the post-modern world, will be those who are mystics."

Connolly, presenting the Jesuit's observations at the 2016 Interfaith conference I had hosted in Halifax, told delegates: "At the time, I don't think the statement resonated with the Catholic world, in the same way as it does today. That insight does not resonate with the Westerner in the 21st-century because we are all so uncomfortable with the whole notion of mystery. We are cerebral people, and so if we are not able to explain an event, through our highly technical minds, then we tend to dismiss it," he said. "We have great difficulty simply standing before the mystery and when we are forced to confront the whole mystery of life, we are unable, like Moses, to just take off our shoes and let the mystery wash over us. And as the mystery washes over us, it tends to unfold before us. But this involves living from our hearts and not from our heads."

You see, mysticism expresses an emotion, and that is not what science can either confirm or deny. It's about becoming one with God as one pursues the insights to the hidden truths.

In the 19th century, William James (1842-1910), proposed that religious experience involves an altogether supernatural domain, somehow inaccessible to science but accessible to the individual human subject. On "Mysticism," a chapter in his book *The Varieties of Religious Experience*, he offers "four marks which, when an experience has them, may justify us in calling it mystical…" The first is ineffability: "it defies expression…its quality must be directly experienced; it cannot be imparted or transferred to others." Second is a "noetic quality": mystical states present themselves as states of knowledge. Thirdly, mystical states are transient; and, fourth, subjects are passive with respect to them: they cannot control their coming and going.[9]

The later post-reformation period also saw the writings of lay visionaries such as Emanuel Swedenborg and William Blake, and the foundation of mystical movements such as the Quakers. Catholic mysticism continued into the modern period with such people as Padre Pio and Thomas Merton.[10]

In the modern era, the scope of the notion and practice of mysticism was broadened to include a range of beliefs and ideologies, and so mysticism can now be found in all religious traditions, from indigenous and folk religions like shamanism, for example, to organized religions including the Abrahamic faiths and Indian religions.

Judaism has had two main kinds of mysticism: Merkabah mysticism and Kabbalah. The former predated the latter, and was focused on visions, particularly those mentioned in the *Book of Ezekiel.* It gets its name from the Hebrew word meaning "chariot," a reference to Ezekiel's vision of a fiery chariot composed of heavenly beings. Kabbalah is a set of esoteric teachings meant to explain the relationship between an unchanging, eternal and mysterious Ein Sof (no end) and the mortal and finite universe (His creation)[11].

India's former Ambassador, Pascal Alan Nazareth, contends that Swami Vivekananda, the Indian monk who became world renowned after he spoke on Hinduism at the World Parliament of Religions at Chicago in 1893, was primarily responsible for Hinduism's revival in pre-independence India as well as in securing for it the status of a world religion and a "spiritual democracy."

In an address he delivered at Benares Hindu University in January 2011, he quoted Swami Vivekananda on what religion actually is: "Religion is not talk, nor doctrine nor theories; nor is it sectarianism. Religion does not consist in erecting temples or building churches or attending public worship. It is the relationship between the individual soul and God. It is not to be found in books or in words or in lectures or in organizations. Religion consists in realization..." Swami Vivekananda is credited with raising Hinduism to the status of a major world religion during the late 19th century.[12]

Buddhism, which originated in India, sometime between the 6th and 4th centuries BCE, seeks liberation from the cycle of rebirth by self-control through meditation and morally just behaviour. Some Buddhist paths aim at a gradual development and transformation of the personality toward Nirvana, like the Theravada stages of enlightenment. Others, like the Japanese Rinzai Zen tradition, emphasize sudden insight, but nevertheless also prescribe intensive meditation and self-restraint."[13]

Classical Sufi scholars have defined Sufism as a science whose objective is the reparation of the heart and turning it away from all else but God.[14]

It all narrows down to plainly being in communion with God. But one of you might say: "Well, I don't know how to pray!" Of course, I relate to that. People are daunted by the prospect of talking to someone that is invisible. But consider the fact that God, as Connolly observes, must be seen from the eye of the heart.

How do you pray? In a silent moment, raise your head and marvel at the stars. Imagine a mysterious force that moves the constellations, keeps the physical constants in their Goldilocks positions so that life for you is made hospitable. Open up the eye of your heart and consider the great wonders of the universe. God is only invisible to the spiritually blind. You will never see Him and live, but you may see his goodness and greatness pass you by. So, as a first step, bow your head and acknowledge that there is a power that is greater than yourself and proclaim: "O God, how great thou art!" That is the hardest part.

Prayer is a humbling act of entering into the truth of things. Be honest with God. Break into tears if you must. Open up your fears, doubts, emotions, hurts, and seek forgiveness and glorify the Lord God. He wants to connect with you.

In Matthew 11:27-28 (NAB), Jesus says: "All things have been handed over to me by my Father. No one knows the Son except the Father, and no one knows the Father except the Son and anyone to whom the Son wishes to reveal him. 'Come to me, all you who labor and are burdened, and I will give you rest.'"

CHAPTER 2

FAITH AND PRAYER

At Holy Mass sometime ago in March, the celebrant, at his homily, said something on faith that I thought was very profound: "The signs and wonders you see as evidence of miraculous action is not what leads you to faith. It is faith that lets you see those signs and experience those wonders." Do you get that?

In a narrative told in the passage below, consider how the "Eyes of Faith" are distinctively independent of the notion of 'belief.'

Professor Joseph Prabhu teaches Philosophy and Religion at California State University, Los Angeles, and is a member of the Board of Trustees for the Parliament of the World's Religions. In a short narrative which he contributed to my recent book *Science and the God Elusion*, he talks about why he stays with the Catholic church.

He firstly recounts the time when he was serving at Mass in a small chapel in Calcutta, as the lone altar boy in the sweltering summer of 1954. "The heat got to me, and I fainted and temporarily lost consciousness," he says. "The next thing I know, a diminutive nun in a white sari with a blue border was splashing some water on me, somewhat angrily and irritably telling me to get up, which, of course, I did. I was in no position then to resist the summons of a (future) saint."

He goes on to say: "Such was my introduction to Mother Teresa of the Missionaries of Charity. I got to meet her fairly often as my father and I would assist her in her humanitarian work. But I cannot say that I ever warmed up to her or her version of Catholicism. This had partly to do with the fact that most of my school education was conducted by a remarkable group of Belgian Jesuits at St. Xavier's School, Calcutta, who transmitted a liberal and, for its time, quite an enlightened version of the faith."

He says the contrast between the two experiences taught him the vital difference between faith and belief. "The language of faith registers a basic spiritual experience and orientation, which the language of belief tries to formulate in propositional or creedal terms. There is, of course, a dialectical and reciprocal relation between faith and belief, but for me faith is primary, while belief, although important, secondary as far as the spiritual life is concerned."

Professor Prabhu says: "I am critically aware of the shortcomings of the Catholic church, an organization showing itself to be an all-too-human institution with its self-aggrandizing-and-protective manner. But the eyes of faith tell me, it (the church) is still, despite its many human failings, the mystical Body of Christ."

The distinction between faith and belief is an important one. "Belief, even though it also involves an element of trust, is primarily but not exclusively, an intellectual matter," he says. "In an age of science, intelligent people will try to make their belief credible and intellectually respectable. But faith moves at a different level: more and more I feel it is a divine gift to which one opens oneself and makes a connection with the Transcendent."

Professor Prabhu says: "I have very little belief that the Catholic Church in its present state can transform itself anytime soon. I do have, however, the faith that the Holy Spirit will, over time, purify and redeem the church. That is a faith that is obviously not provable."

Speaking of what is and what is not provable, there is apparently, now, scientific proof of faith being "hardwired" into the human condition.

McHargue, who is also host of the popular television series *Ask Science Mike*, posits that spirituality and religion are rooted in the brain in the same way that thoughts and feelings are. His book, afore-mentioned, reveals how the latest in neuroscience, physics and biology help us understand God, faith and ourselves. Scholars of neuroscience are, in fact, proposing that religion is genetically "hardwired" into the human condition, according to recent scientific research.

McHargue tells us the two basic brain networks that work together to make God real in the minds of humans like us are, understandably, complex and explain much about our faith. "It explains why people with higher activity in their frontal lobes will be drawn to apologetics or theology – they want to know how God works. On the other hand, people with higher activity in their limbic systems will know God through feelings and have little concern with rational justifi-cations for God's existence. They know God because they feel God." [1]

So, it's no great second guess why billions of people of faith today testify to the fact that God has, indeed, been emotionally satisfying and has intervened in the egregious moments of their lives. The brutality of the communist leaders of China, the former Soviet Union and Cambodia, knew it in their gut that the shutting down of churches and mosques would fail to demolish the inner soulful faith of their people.

In the years of ideological tyranny and radicalization in the former communist states, a section of Christians and Muslims may have worshipped in underground churches and mosques, but millions worshipped through a mystical experience.

Professor Richard Dawkins, the most prominent atheist on the planet at this time, is, understandably, baffled with this growing sense of spirituality that springs forth in mystical ways. He mourns the fact that while great scientists who profess religion become harder to find through the twentieth century, there are nevertheless good scientists who are sincerely religious in the full, traditional sense.

He speaks of Peacocke, Stannard and Polkinghorne who have all either won the Templeton Prize or are on the Templeton Board of Trustees. He writes: "After amicable discussions with all of them, both in public and in private, I remain baffled, not so much by their belief in a cosmic lawgiver of some kind, as by their belief in the details of the Christian faith: resurrection, forgiveness of sin and all."[2]

Faith is the cornerstone of one's acknowledgement of the omniscience of God – the elusive God, whose face you cannot see although you see his goodness pass you by. It is through the eyes of faith that you come face-to-face with the Creator. It is through faith that you experience God.

Let's examine the topic from a Christian lens. In scripture, we are told Jesus often urged his followers to believe through faith. In one of the most widely known scriptures, Matthew 17:20 NAB, Jesus said, "Amen, I say to you, if you have faith the size of a mustard seed, you will say to this mountain, 'Move from here to there,' and it will move. Nothing will be impossible for you."

On a stormy night, Jesus exhorts Peter to leave the boat and walk up to him upon the waters. Peter does as he is told but as his faith crumbles and he is about to drown, Jesus grabs him and despairs, saying: "O ye of little faith. Why did you doubt?"

After His resurrection from the dead, Jesus meets with the disciple Thomas - who had refused to believe the resurrection story - and shows him his wounds, urging the disciple to put his hand in his side. Thomas looks up at him and proclaims: "My Lord and my God." Jesus said to him, "Have you come to believe because you have seen me? Blessed are those who have not seen and have believed." (John 20:29 NAB)

When He walked this earth, Jesus calmed the storms, gave sight to the blind, cleansed the lepers, raised Lazarus from the dead, changed water to wine, fed the crowds of 5000 people, cast out demons. But throughout the New Testament, we are told that Jesus often withdrew to the mountains to pray. (Luke 5:16)

So, the faithful turn to prayer because it is the most personal way to experience God. The Lord's Prayer is a model of a prayer of praise, submission to God's will, reliance upon Him and supplication for forgiveness and deliverance. In my own experience, it is through prayer that a sterling faith evolves. It's about seeing with the heart and acknowledging that there is something greater than ourselves. Prayer is an act of humility.

In our time, we've heard of the many miracles at Fatima in Portugal and Lourdes in France. These are the healing shrines of the Christian Virgin Mary. The many devout Christians returning after supplicating at these shrines tell you that there are, for example, many crutches hanging in the grotto of Lourdes, testifying to the fact that many who came lame, left whole.

In a treatise titled "Prayer and Healing: A medical and scientific perspective on randomized controlled trials," published in the *Indian Journal Of Psychiatry* 2009,[3] meditation has been found to produce a clinically significant reduction in ambulatory blood pressure,[4] to reduce heart rate,[5] to result in cardio-respiratory synchronization,[6] to alter levels of melatonin and serotonin,[7] to boost the immune response,[8] to reduce stress and promote positive mood states, to reduce anxiety and pain and enhance self-esteem.[9]

Scientists, however, dismiss faith healing as pseudoscience. The American Cancer Society states "available scientific evidence does not support claims that faith healing can actually cure physical ailments."[10]

But, then, that argument brings us back to square one. Science cannot prove or disprove God because He is not a scientific question. That is a theological and philosophical one. So, it's only natural that from a scientific perspective, faith healing is unexplained, and incomprehensible.

It's quite like the story of the Bumble Bee. Scientists tell us that according to the laws of physics, the insect should not be able to fly. But the Bumble bee does not know that. So, it flies regardless. Scientists recognise that there are placebo effects in healing, but have trouble making sense of that.

The universe is one enigmatic mystery. The eminent scientist Albert Einstein always stood aside from secular scientists saying his response to the mysterious force that moves the constellations has been one of awe. "My religiosity consists in a humble admiration of the infinitely superior spirit that reveals itself in the little that we, with our weak and transitory understanding, can comprehend of reality.[11]"

So, never mind what science has to say on this matter. According to a *Newsweek* poll released some years ago, 72 percent of Americans said they believe that praying to God can cure someone, even if science says the person has an incurable disease.[12]

In Mark 5:25-34 (NAB), we are told of the story of the woman who touched the cloak of Jesus and was healed:

> "There was a woman afflicted with hemor-rhages for twelve years. She had suffered greatly at the hands of many doctors and had spent all that she had. Yet she was not helped but only grew worse. She had heard about Jesus and came up behind him in the crowd and touched his cloak. She said, "If I but touch his clothes, I shall be cured." Immediately her flow of blood dried up. She felt in her body that she was healed of her affliction.
>
> Jesus, aware at once that power had gone out from him, turned around in the crowd and asked, "Who has touched my clothes?" But his disciples said to him, "You see how the crowd is pressing

upon you, and yet you ask, 'Who touched me?'"
And he looked around to see who had done it.

The woman, realizing what had happened to her, approached in fear and trembling. She fell down before Jesus and told him the whole truth. He said to her, "Daughter, your faith has saved you. Go in peace and be cured of your affliction."

When he walked this earth, Jesus healed the leper, the blind, the crippled and so many others merely saying "Go your faith has saved you."

In Mark 10:50-52 (NAB), we read:

He threw aside his cloak, sprang up, and came to Jesus. Jesus said to him in reply, "What do you want me to do for you?" The blind man replied to him, "Master, I want to see." Jesus told him, "Go your way; your faith has saved you." Immediately he received his sight and followed him on the way.

CHAPTER 3

SUFFERING AND DEATH

Those that recall that famous line: *It is well with my soul* might also be familiar with the story of Horatio Gates Spafford, who after a string of egregious tragedies in the family wrote that famous hymn. His story is presented in the second part of this book and what that chilling narrative tells you is that you cannot be a fair-weather friend of God.

I have grown up listening to my father sing that hymn and rock my younger siblings in his arms to sleep for those many years. But it was only several years later that I got to learn of Spafford's story and his profound Christian faith which inspired him to write those famous lines.

When peace, like a river, attendeth my way,
When sorrows like sea billows roll;
Whatever my lot, Thou hast taught me to say,
It is well, it is well with my soul.

Spafford's trials and tribulations have been likened to the miseries of Job in the Old Testament of the Christian bible. Job is presented as a virtuous and prosperous family man who is beset by Satan in God's oversight, with horrendous disasters that take away all that he holds dear, including his offspring, his health, and his property.

He struggles to understand the purpose of his suffering, and while he curses the day he was born, he stops short of proclaiming God as an unjust Creator. Job is finally blessed with restoration of his former wealth and with seven sons and three daughters.

So, what is it about suffering and death that makes some turn away from God?

In 1348, the bubonic plague or Black Death swept across Europe, wiping out a third of Europe's population, at the time, or approximately 75 million to 200 million lives.[1] The 1918 Spanish flu infected 500 million people around the world and resulted in the deaths of close to 50 million people.[2] In the last century, World War 1 saw casualties of 40 million lives, and World War II was the deadliest military conflict in history.[3] On a less appalling scale, natural calamity from tsunamis, droughts, earthquakes, heat waves, floods and landslides have wiped away hundreds of thousands of people in the last 20 years.

And now, the coronavirus (Covid-19). It began its treacherous journey across the world in China sometime in December 2019 and has swept away some 2.79 million lives, as reported in the middle of March 2021. In its course, it changed life for people on the planet.

Indeed, these may have all been natural calamities – although scientists and apologists have not altogether ruled out human agency in some of these appalling disasters and speak of the impending consequences of climate change impacting the universe some decades down the line.[4]

But what's increasingly troubling, really, is that outside the realm of natural calamities, suffering and death are an everyday occurrence on our planet, and all of that ongoing tragedy is provoked by mankind's lust and greed, notions of supremacy and the drive to conquer, bringing into the world poverty and strife, hateful ideology, violence and destruction, conflict and war, often orchestrated for the cause of nationhood and religion, both of which are accidents of birth.

So, it's perfectly natural to ask 'why does a loving God allow suffering and death.' The short answer is that no one is going to pretend to know the mind of God, but science and theology can, at best, make some sense of why suffering and death prevail.

Charles Darwin wrote in *The Origin of Species*: "In looking at nature, it is most necessary to keep the foregoing considerations always in mind, never to forget that every single organic being around us may be said to be striving to the utmost to increase in numbers; that each lives by a struggle at some period of its life, that heavy destruction inevitably falls either on the young or old during each generation or at recurrent intervals."[5] That, of course, is a secular, scientific view.

Suffering, as Christian theologians agree, is inevitable in everyone's lifetime as a consequence of the fall of man. This refers to the fall of Adam – the first man. The theological response to the question about why God allows suffering and death is addressed in revealed scripture: "For the wages of sin is death, but the gift of God is eternal life in Christ Jesus our Lord." (Romans 6:23 NAB). That is why Christians call themselves Easter people.

So, is sin the harbinger of death? According to Christian scripture, death has come through Adam and life through Christ. "Therefore, just as through one person sin entered the world, and through sin, death, and thus death came to all, inasmuch as all sinned." (Romans 5:12, NAB)

In Ephesians 2:3 (NAB), we read: "All of us once lived among them in the desires of our flesh, following the wishes of the flesh and the impulses, and we were by nature children of wrath, like the rest." Theologians therefore agree that with Adam's rebellion against God, all of his descendants are regarded as people wanting a life without God. The theological deduction thus concludes that since God is the author of life, death is the natural penalty of wanting life without its Creator.

Well, how do other faiths perceive suffering and death?

In his *Deer Park Sermon*, Buddha expounded his first teaching of the Four Noble Truths, which explains the problem of suffering and misery in the world and offers a solution. Those four noble truths are: 1. There is suffering. In other words, suffering is a given. 2. There is a cause of suffering 3. There is cessation of suffering 4. There is a path to the cessation of suffering.[6]

Hinduism considers the suffering of individuals in a broader context of a cosmic cycle of birth, life, destruction and rebirth.

Death in Islam is the termination of worldly life and the beginning of afterlife. It is seen as the separation of the *soul* from the body and its transfer from this world to the afterlife. In fact, belief in an afterlife is one of the six articles of faith in Islam. [7]

The Christian doctrine on death, however, is, in fact, the cornerstone of its gospel. The coming of Jesus Christ to redeem sinners and connect us all to God and his death upon a cross to pay man's debt incurred by sin is a theology that must be understood with divine grace. "For God so loved the world that he gave his only Son, so that everyone who believes in him might not perish but might have eternal life." (John 3:16, NAB) The resurrection of Jesus brings victory over death and holds out the promise of salvation. Therefore, the acclamation in 1 Corinthians 15:55 (NAB): "Where, O death, is your victory? Where, O death, is your sting??"

So, how does the God experience through faith or in its absence, manifest itself in suffering and death?

Let me illustrate this with two examples: One of the most widely believed episodes in the life of Charles Darwin, is that the death of his daughter, Annie, in 1851 caused the end of Darwin's belief in Christianity, and, according to some versions, ended his attendance at church on Sundays. That reflects the absence of faith manifesting itself in suffering and death.

Contrast that narrative with another experience. I do recall a dear Muslim friend of mine narrating the death of his young brother and of how much grief that brought about in the extended family. However, he said: "My father was completely calm and serene at the time. To those who comforted him, he said: 'God has given and God has taken.'"

In Horatio Spafford's story told in the second part of this book, we are told he lost almost everything dearest to his heart, not to speak of six of his children and almost all of his wealth, through a string of tragedies. His response was to glorify God, composing the famous hymn: *It is well with my soul.*

Now these two narratives reflect the sterling presence of faith, manifesting itself in the face of death.

So, what this says is that if one must be truly alive, one must factor suffering in our lives and that when you attach meaning and purpose to your suffering, no matter how pernicious, that suffering will be ephemeral.

A man of faith must reconcile with the truth that this world is not our home and that when death comes, we know life is changed, not taken away. So, for Christians, that is the cornerstone of the God experience. The witnessing of Jesus' death and his resurrection on the third day introduces hope that one day suffering will be relegated to history. "For just as in Adam all die, so too in Christ shall all be brought to life." (1 Corinthians 15:22, NAB)

Bible scriptures have been used throughout the

centuries as a way of making sense of death. In John's gospel, Martha speaks to Jesus about the death of her brother Lazarus.

Martha said to Jesus, "Lord, if you had been here, my brother would not have died. [But] even now I know that whatever you ask of God, God will give you." Jesus said to her, "Your brother will rise." Martha said to him, "I know he will rise, in the resurrection on the last day." Jesus told her, "I am the resurrection and the life; whoever believes in me, even if he dies, will live, and everyone who lives and believes in me will never die. Do you believe this?" She said to him, "Yes, Lord. I have come to believe that you are the Messiah, the Son of God, the one who is coming into the world."

Jesus said to her, "Did I not tell you that if you believe you will see the glory of God?" So they took away the stone. And Jesus raised his eyes and said, "Father, I thank you for hearing me. I know that you always hear me; but because of the crowd here I have said this, that they may believe that you sent me." And when he had said this, he cried out in a loud voice, "Lazarus, come out!" The dead man came out, tied hand and foot with burial bands, and his face was wrapped in a cloth. So Jesus said to them, "Untie him and let him go. (John 11:21-27, 40-44 NAB)

There is comfort in Revelation 21:4 (NAB) "He will wipe every tear from their eyes, and there shall be no more death or mourning, wailing or pain, [for] the old order has passed away."

Philippians 3:20-21 (NAB) speaks of citizenship in heaven. "But our citizenship is in heaven, and from it we also await a savior, the Lord Jesus Christ. He will change our lowly body to conform with his glorified body by the power that enables him also to bring all things into subjection to himself."

CHAPTER 4

PURPOSE OF LIFE

Where Have We Come From and Where Are We Going are two questions that have vexed writers, painters and intellects of all shades throughout history. Those two questions are, in fact, part of the title of a painting by French artist Paul Gauguin. The painting, *Where Do We Come From? What Are We? Where Are We Going?* is dated 1897, was created in Tahiti and is in the Museum of Fine Arts in Boston, Massachusetts. Gauguin studied Catholic liturgy as a young lad in a school outside Orleans whose catechism, at the time, centred on these profound questions.

The painting has three major figure groups illustrating the questions posed in the title. The three women with a child represent the beginning of life; the middle group symbolizes the daily existence of young adulthood; and in the final group, according to the artist, "an old woman approaching death appears reconciled and resigned to her thoughts." At her feet, "a strange white bird...represents the futility of words"

The blue idol in the background apparently represents what Gauguin described as "the Beyond."[1]

Where Have We Come From and Where Are We Going is also the theme of Dan Brown's recent novel *Origin*. Edmond Kirsch, a billionaire philanthropist, computer scientist, futurist and strident atheist – who is a key character in the plot, meets with a Roman Catholic Bishop, a Jewish Rabbi and a Muslim Imam – all of them members of the Parliament of World Religions - and tells them that he has a revolutionary discovery to unfold. They are horrified when they learn that he is soon to reveal in a presentation something that will provide the answers to two of life's most important questions: "Where did we come from?" and "Where are we going?" The objective, they soon learn, is to end the age of religion and usher in an age of science.

Finally, days later, hundreds of millions of viewers witness on screen a demonstration by Kirsch of how by simulating the famous Miller-Urey experiment and coupling it with various components employing the laws of physics and entropy, along with E-Wave's ability to digitally speed forward time, science can recreate what he believes is the moment of abiogenesis.[2] It refers to the original evolution of life from inorganic substance. Well, in Dan Brown's book

Origin, this is the billionaire's proof that humanity was created by natural events. It's a brilliant novel. But, what has science to say about the Miller-Urey experiment. The foregoing passages present a viewpoint.

I did not think about these profound questions when I was twenty. That's why they say youth is wasted on the young. In some of the testimonies that are reproduced in this book, you notice that atheism kicks in when one is young and foolish.

But when I was fifty, I began to see futility in worldly pursuit. I was becoming increasingly aware that life is meaningless if I did not understand that there was a purpose to it. In one of the testimonies, presented in this book, Dr. Francis Collins, the world's top scientist today and a former atheist, talks about his pursuit of God in later years. The tipping point, he says, came about when he was turning the pages of C.S. Lewis's influential book *Mere Christianity*.

He writes: "In the first two or three pages, I realized that my arguments against faith were really those of a school boy... I had imagined that faith and reason were at opposite poles. And here was this deep intellectual who was convincing me quickly page by page that reason and faith go hand in hand."[3]

So, let's put fiction behind us for now and examine

the question: How did life evolve?

Dr Gerald Schroeder, a prominent scientist and author of the book *The Hidden Face of God*, tells us that in 1953 when the Miller-Urey experiment was investigating whether chemical self-organization could have been possible in a primordial ocean, there was initial euphoria over the results that might provide the key to how life began. But, he says subsequent experiments failed to extend those findings.

"We can predict all the elements used in life but there is no indication that we can predict amino acids joining together in chains of hundreds of thousands of units to form proteins and then proteins combining into symbiotic relationships we refer to as life. When in 1953, Stanley Miller, then a graduate student at The University of Chicago, produced a few amino acids through purely random reactions among chemicals found naturally throughout the universe, the scientific community felt the problem of life's origin had been solved. Far from it. Subsequent experiments failed to extend his results. Thermodynamics favours disorder over order. Attempting to get those amino acids to join into any sort of complex molecules has been one long study in failure. The emergence of the specialized complexity of life, even in its simplest forms, remains a bewildering mystery."[4]

In short, he posits, that attempts to get amino acids to join into any sort of complex molecules – as the Miller-Urey experiment sought to do - has been one long study in failure.

Now let's back track some hundred and sixty plus years ago when in 1859 Charles Darwin released his revolutionary theory of evolution in his book *Origin of Species*. There was great euphoria then as well. Then, in time, a section of the scientific world stretched out his theory significantly to make a case for organisms evolving from elemental atoms, which, instructed by a self-creating universe of natural laws, evolved into living tissues. That, in irreverent silence, was an attempt by a section of the scientific world to ignore the first cause argument - one that infers from causal logic, a self-creator or God as the cause of the universe.

Charles Darwin's famous theory of Natural Selection may now be one of the cornerstones of modern biology, but keep this in mind – Darwin, in the final editions of his book wrote: "Nevertheless, all living things have much in common, in their chemical com-

position, their germinal vesicles, their cellular structure
and their laws of growth and reproduction..... Therefore, I should infer from analogy, that probably all the
organic human beings which have ever lived on this
earth, have descended from some one primordial form,
into which life was breathed."[5]

In the subsequent edition, Darwin enters the
phrase "by the Creator" to follow the word "breathed."
In so doing, Darwin acknowledged the first cause.

It is very natural to respond with some perplexity
to this complex proposition of a self-creating universe.
The probability of obtaining even a single functioning
protein by a serendipitous combination of amino acids
- a hypothesis the British astronomer Sir Fred Hoyle
had scoffed at - is what makes acceptance of theories of
the origin of life dubious. Will the passage of time
change the perspective? Let's see.

Stephen Weppner, Professor of Physics at Eckerd
College, Florida, tells me it is well-known that science,
like religion, is a paradigm, so a theist should not worry
at any moment about science challenging faith. "And if
science is only a paradigm that can change, it thus
screams its limited ability to observe truth," he says.
"There is no disagreement about the fact that religion
can be couched in the same language. But science is not
special. It is one more human endeavor that is open to

the same limitations and faults as any other human endeavor, including religion."

Dr. Weppner also tells me that fifty years ago the argument was that scientists will never explain why flowers bloom because it is the purview of God. "But scientists found out how flowers bloom eighteen years ago. Likewise, someday science may put amino acids together to form a complex molecule. That should not diminish God. Like evolution itself, man's understanding of God's creation is a work in progress."

Indeed, science has told us what it knows from what it has seen. But the truth may be elusive because science cannot tell us with empirical evidence what it cannot see. So, the answers to the profound questions man has posed – the questions about where we have come from and where are we going - lie behind a closed door. Science is silent on that.

So, "where have we come from?" is a mystical pursuit for some, inspired by revealed scripture in the Holy Books, and for others, the path to the truth is via philosophical and theological insights.

The Christian narrative on "where we have come from?" is found in the opening lines of Genesis. "In the beginning, when God created the heavens and the earth—and the earth was without form or shape, with darkness over the abyss and a mighty wind sweeping over the waters—then God said: Let there be light, and there was light. God saw that the light was good. God then separated the light from the darkness. God called the light 'day,' and the darkness he called 'night.' Evening came, and morning followed—the first day. (Genesis 1:1-5, NAB)

Genesis 1:6-25 is the narrative of creation and Genesis 1:26 (NAB) proclaims: "Then God said: Let us make human beings in our image, after our likeness. Let them have dominion over the fish of the sea, the birds of the air, the tame animals, all the wild animals, and all the creatures that crawl on the earth."

At a presentation at the third Spiritual Diversity Conference held in Halifax in 2016, Syed Mustaffa al-Qazwini, President of the Shia Muslim Council of Southern California, told delegates, the Quran states: "Humankind, we have created you from a single cell of male and female and made you into tribes so you may recognize one another."

Let's examine the cosmological view from the point of view of Hindu philosophy. Commenting on the topic at my first seminar on *Science and the God Elusion* - my recent book - Pascal Alan Nazareth, India's former Ambassador said this: "The basic thought in respect of the cosmological view - in Indian philosophy and theology - is captured in the words: *Tat Twam Asi* which means *Thou Art That*. What it implies is that the Creator is a part of His own creation or of what we call the soul within us. He is the cosmic spirit, the universal cosmic energy which pervades the universe and all that you see is a manifestation of that energy."

So, let's move on. In discussing the question: "Where Are We Going?" let me provide a Christian perspective again.

On September 11, 2001, Islamic jihadists hijacked planes and crashed them into the Twin Towers in New York. The world watched the unfolding tragedy in shock as people jumped out of windows to their death. The official casualty toll was 2,996 dead and more than 6,000 others wounded. At the time, Americans were all asking the same question: "Why does God allow tragedy and suffering."

The American Christian evangelist Billy Graham, speaking at the National Cathedral in Washington D.C. on September 14, three days after the 9/11 tragedy, told crowds gathered to hear him: "I have to confess I do not know the answer. The story does not end with the cross, for Easter points us beyond the tragedy of the cross to the empty tomb."[6]

Let me insert an explanatory note to Graham's narrative. His reference to Easter and the empty tomb is a recall of the resurrection of Jesus Christ from the dead, three days after his crucifixion. The scriptures tell us that just as in Adam we all die, in Christ, we shall all be resurrected.

In an earlier chapter, I narrated the story of Jesus raising up Lazarus from the dead, after telling his sister Martha: "I am the resurrection and the life; whoever believes in me, even if he dies, will live." (John 11:25, NAB)

The testimonies by so many atheists who have converted to Christianity tell us that the turning point in their search for purpose had come from an inspirational grasp of the significance of the crucifixion of Jesus which wiped out the sin of man by an act of forgiveness, thus opening the way to salvation and eternal life.

Dr. Collins told an audience at the opening of the BioLogos (Science and Faith) conference in 2019 how the cogent arguments laid out in C.S. Lewis's *Mere Christianity* brought him to realise that reason can take you to the point where you see that God is very real. He ends his presentation, making the point that God's holiness can reconcile with our sinfulness "....only through the person of Jesus Christ who not only claimed to know God but to be God and who in this uplifting, sacrificial act died on the cross and then rose from the dead to provide this bridge between my imperfections and God's holiness in a way that made more sense than I ever dreamed it could."[7]

Likewise, other former atheists have affirmed the experience of an absence-of-purpose which germinates under the notion that this is a godless world. Man's quest for an answer to why we are here is foundational to discovering purpose.

In much the same way, it's quite natural to ask the question that if life began in a primordial ocean with organisms evolving from elemental atoms and then, instructed by a self-creating universe of natural laws, suddenly flashed into living tissues, why would human life be sacred at all? If then, any credence is to be given to this serendipity in an evolution theory that does not accept a first cause, why would we call the destruction of human life abominable?

A world without God, is a world in chaos, in moral decline where right and wrong is a perspective. This moral decline has been gradual through the centuries, but what we see today perhaps took root during the dark days of the post world war depression. Consequentially, what followed was a bouncing back to a consuming world inspired by what was being described as the emerging Woodstock culture of the sixties. That movement brought about the liberation of self and the casting off of restraint. Most young teenagers today in college are dreaming of piling up millions. A Hollywood star might rank first among some of their heroes, and Jesus might come in third. The grain of moral values has eroded to an extent that the recent American elections which ejected Donald Trump out of the White House put "character and decency" on the top rung of the Presidential morality ladder – a stark reminder to brash upstarts that winning the day is not about you. So long as you believe you're in charge of your life, you will be drifting further from the truth.

When I was a young lad, I remember dad singing the song *I'm just a gigolo* and somehow, even to this day, I have not forgotten the chorus lines:

> *There will come a day when youth will pass away*
> *What will they say about me?*
> *When the end comes, I know*
> *They were just the gigolos*
> *Life goes on, without me.*

In conclusion, let me say this: Life, suffering and death can only begin to present meaning, from a Christian point of view when you see the goodness of God pass you by. But how can you see the goodness of God pass you by? There's a response to that in Luke 17:20-21 (NAB): "Asked by the Pharisees when the kingdom of God would come, he said in reply, 'The coming of the kingdom of God cannot be observed, and no one will announce, 'Look, here it is,' or, 'There it is.' For behold, the kingdom of God is among you.'"

Close your eyes and let the mystery wash over you. Harden not your heart, so you may see the wonder of creation and know that it's inane to think that something could come from nothing. Try some humility and recognise the fact that there must be something greater than yourself – especially given the fact that you can do nothing about death. That's when you rest in the knowledge that suffering can be fleeting and that death is the last enemy that the resurrection of Christ claims victory over.

So, where are we going? The answer is intrinsic in the lines: In death, life is changed, not taken away. "Where, O death, is your victory? Where, O death, is your sting?" (1 Corinthians 15:55, NAB). Jesus is the resurrection and the life. The one who believes in Him will live, even though they die.

CHAPTER 5

Sin, Free Will and the Resurrection

In the film *The Two Popes,* a profound statement on sin comes from the character playing Pope Francis. In a conversation, Francis tells emeritus Pope Benedict: "Sin is a wound, not a stain. It must be healed." That is one of the most profound observations on sin that I have heard, and it's so contextual when you think of the Creator as a compassionate and forgiving God.

In a religious context, sin is a transgression against divine law. While sins are generally actions, any thought, word, or deed considered immoral or shameful might be termed "sinful."[1]

The severity of sin, which is a violation of the moral law, is the fundamental yard stick - in the tenets of most religions which conform to the belief of an afterlife - by which the Creator shall judge man's worthiness for eternal salvation. Theologically, sinning indulges one's own lower nature to turn the mirror of one's heart away from God.

In Christian liturgy, sin was the cause of the fall of

man in the garden of Eden and the forerunner of death. The New Testament, as aforementioned, calls death "the last enemy" (1 Corinthians 15:26, NAB).

Augustine of Hippo, who is Doctor of the Church, wrote extensively on the impossibility of a sinless life without Christ, and the necessity of Christ's grace. He is quoted as famously saying: "*non possum non peccare*" which is "I cannot not sin."[2]

Pelagius opposed Augustine's doctrine. The view that mankind can avoid sinning, and that humans can freely choose to obey God's commandments, stands at the core of Pelagian teaching. Pelagius stressed human autonomy and freedom of the will. He said humans were not wounded by Adam's sin and were perfectly able to fulfill the law without divine aid. He was declared a heretic by the Council of Ephesus in 431. His interpretation of a doctrine of free will became known as Pelagianism.[3]

Judaism regards the violation of any of the 613 commandments as a sin but teaches that to sin is a part of life since there is no perfect man and everyone has an inclination to do evil in his youth.[4]

Baha'u'llah, the founder of the Baha'i faith, wrote: "Watch over yourselves, for the Evil One is lying in wait, ready to entrap you. Gird yourselves against his wicked devices, and, led by the light of the name of the

All-Seeing God, make your escape from the darkness that surroundeth you."[5]

Sin, death and the resurrection are the cornerstones of the Christian faith. But of course, we cannot discuss sin without a reference to the problem of evil, the conundrum of free will, death and God's forgiveness.

It's not uncommon to reason that the presence of trial and tribulation, the evil of war and destruction, oppression and injustice upon the weak and innocent would be adequate proof that a loving Creator does not exist. But consider the fact that despite the trial and tribulation, the evil of war and destruction, oppression and injustice upon the weak and innocent, we witness every day how the human race counters evil with good, war with peace, oppression with justice, hatred with love. In our time, we have seen how the mighty have fallen, blood thirsty dictatorships have crumbled, the oppressed have found refuge, the poor are fed and hatred has been blunted.

Merton, suggests that this would never have been possible without the merciful love of God, pouring out His grace upon mankind. That is because there can, at least, be no doubt about the authors of hate, avarice and injustice, all of which sow the seeds of war and destruction.

So, God cannot be the author of evil. When you look around and see the beauty of the mountains, the expanse of the seas, consider the order in the universe, unravel the mystery of the physical constants which make our planet hospitable to life, or when we witness the birthing of a child, the instinct of a mother, the flight of a sparrow, the blooming of a sunflower, reason prompts you to conclude that an omniscient and omnipotent God alone would be the first cause, a divine Creator Who embodies holiness and an all embracing love. And by reason, too, you know, He cannot be the author of evil.

The problem of evil, by deduction therefore, lies elsewhere and might have originated in the garden of Eden when man and woman cashing in on the gift of free will would have sinned, prompting God to evict them out of paradise.

Free will and predestination have been debated since the time of the early Church fathers, who emphasised man's freedom of choice alongside God's determinative activity. Pelagius (354-418) over-emphasised human potential. Saint Augustine (354-430) reacted against Pelagianism with a doctrine of predestination, election and efficient grace.

The questions that vex the predetermination thinker are, firstly, how can man choose without impinging on God's action and, second, how can God act without impinging on man's choices?

What do scientists say about free will and predetermination?

Like the Dutch philosopher Spinoza, Einstein was a strict determinist who believed that human behavior was completely determined by causal laws. He refuted the chance aspect of quantum theory, famously telling Niels Bohr: "God does not play dice with the universe."[6] In letters sent to physicist Max Born, Einstein revealed his belief in causal relationships. Bohr believed that there are truly random activities within the universe - at least at the quantum level - and argued in favour, therefore, of the existence of free will. Einstein proposed that Free Will is a concept outside the realm of physics and dismissed the chance aspect of quantum theory.

If free will does not truly exist, that would seemingly place the onus of all action on the Creator. However, we have argued that God cannot be the originator of evil from evidence of his Creation. That then opens up the debate as to who, then, is the author of sin and the problem of evil. Perhaps an understanding of the con-

undrum of free will and predestination can cast a light
on that.

What is the view from religionists?

There are two forms of theological determinism.
Strong theological determinism is based on the concept
of a Creator deity dictating all events in history. In
other words: "Everything that happens has been predestined by an omniscient, omnipotent divinity."[7]

The second form, weak theological determinism, is
based on the concept of divine foreknowledge and that,
because God's omniscience is perfect, what God knows
about the future will inevitably happen, which means,
consequently, that the future is already fixed.[8] This view
holds that God, who has foreknowledge of that action,
does not affect the outcome. The belief is that God's
providence is "compatible" with voluntary choice.

The concept of theological determinism has its origins within the Bible as well as within the Christian
church. A major theological dispute at the time of the
sixteenth century drove a distinct division in ideas -
with an argument between two eminent thinkers of the
time, Desiderius Erasmus and Martin Luther, a leading
Protestant Reformer.

Erasmus, in *Discourses on the Freedom of the Will,*

explained his belief that God created human beings en-
dowed with free will. He maintained that, despite the
fall of Adam and Eve, freedom was not taken away. As
a result of this, humans had the ability to do good or
evil.

Luther, conversely, attacked the idea in *On the
Bondage of the Will.* He recognised that the issue of
autonomy lay at the heart of religious dissension. He
depicted an image of humanity manipulated through
sin. Humans, for Luther, know what is morally right
but are unable to attain it. He asserted that humans
thus must give up aspiring to do good in their fallen
state and by their own power, as only by this could
salvation be granted. This is reflected in the reformation doctrine that asserts that salvation is by faith
alone and not achieved by meritorious good works.
Luther also believed that the fall of Adam and Eve, as
told in the Bible, supported this notion.[9]

Theologians of the Roman Catholic Church uni-
versally embrace the idea of free will but generally do
not view free will as existing apart from or in contra-
diction to grace. According to the Roman Catholic
Church, "To God, all moments of time are present in
their immediacy. When therefore he establishes his
eternal plan of "predestination," he includes in it each

person's free response to his grace."[10]

A view of the Catholic position can also be seen from Paul's notes to Romans 8:29-30 (NAB): "For those he foreknew he also predestined to be conformed to the image of his Son, so that he might be the firstborn among many brothers. And those he predestined he also called; and those he called he also justified; and those he justified he also glorified."

In libertarian freedom, an action is free if when the action is performed – all things being just what they are - the agent could have done otherwise. So, you make undetermined choices. In compatabilist freedom, a man's action is compatible with God's oversight and control. In the Old Testament narrative of Genesis, Joseph's exile, some theologians say, was driven not by the vile plot of his brothers, but by God's decision to send him to Egypt. His brothers meant evil against him – they sold him into slavery to the Ishmaelites who then brought Joseph to Egypt - but God sent Joseph to that country for the greater good. In Genesis 45:5 (NAB), we read: "But now do not be distressed, and do not be angry with yourselves for having sold me here. It was really for the sake of saving lives that God sent me here ahead of you."

In his missives to the Romans, Paul speaks of God's desire to extend his mercy just as widely as the infection of sin. Salvation is not by works. "And they also, if they do not remain in unbelief, will be grafted in, for God is able to graft them in again." (Romans 11:23, NAB)

In *Discovering Islam*, with reference to free will, the author Syed Moustafa Al Qazwini says there are two schools of thought: "One called the 'compulsionist' (Jabr) holds that human beings do not have the freedom of choice. Every decision, utterance and action a person performs has been predestined since the time of creation. Compulsionists believe that the faithful have no choice in their faith. Likewise, the unfaithful also have no choice but not to believe in God. They maintain that everything is unalterable and predetermined.

"The second school of thought who believe in free will (Tafwid) declare that human beings are masters over their own acts. This notion is in concordance with the Quran which states: 'The truth is from your Lord. So whoever wills, let him believe and whoever wills, let him disbelieve.' "[11] (18:29)

Syed Qazwini then contends that human beings have the freedom to act, but they must bear the moral responsibility and consequences of their own actions.

What is the view of the philosopher?

The Stanford Encyclopedia of Philosophy has an erudite essay on the subject, but let me quote an excerpt which seeks to make a logical deduction from the point of view of alternative possibilities.

The argument on determinism and alternative possibilities runs alongside the following deductions:

a. If someone acts out of her own will, then she could have done otherwise.
b. If determinism is true, no one can do otherwise, than one actually does.
c. Therefore, if determinism is true, no one acts out of her own free will.[12]

Human frailty tells us that although man knows what is morally right, he is unable to act righteously and, therefore, as Luther proposed, should give up aspiring to do good in his fallen state and by his own power, as only by this could salvation be granted. This is reflected in the reformation doctrine that asserts that salvation is by faith alone and not achieved by meritorious good works. The fall of Adam and Eve, as told in the Bible, and as Luther affirms, conforms to this notion.

If then, the argument that free will is an endowment to man from God and human frailty does not permit man to act righteously at all times, then, by deduction, man is the author of the problem of evil. That opens up the niggling question: If man then is the author of the problem of evil, why cannot God put an end to it?

Daniel Defoe, author of *Robinson Crusoe*, narrates a conversation with his man Friday which provides an insight to the question.

> "Well," says Friday, "but you say God is so strong, so great; is He not much strong, much might as the devil?"
>
> "Yes, yes," says I, "Friday, God is stronger than the devil—God is above the devil, and therefore we pray to God to tread him down under our feet, and enable us to resist his temptations and quench his fiery darts."
>
> "But," says he again, "if God much stronger, much might as the wicked devil, why God no kill the devil, so make him no more do wicked?"
>
> I was strangely surprised at this question; and, after all, though I was now an old man, yet I was but a young doctor, and ill qualified for a casuist or a

solver of difficulties; and at first I could not tell what to say; so I pretended not to hear him, and asked him what he said; but he was too earnest for an answer to forget his question, so that he repeated it in the very same broken words as above.

By this time I had recovered myself a little, and I said, "God will at last punish him severely; he is reserved for the judgment, and is to be cast into the bottomless pit, to dwell with everlasting fire." This did not satisfy Friday; but he returns upon me, repeating my words, "'*Reserve at last!*' me no understand—but why not kill the devil now; not kill great ago?"

"You may as well ask me," said I, "why God does not kill you or me, when we do wicked things here that offend Him—we are preserved to repent and be pardoned." He mused some time on this. "Well, well," says he, mighty affectionately, "that well—so you, I, devil, all wicked, all preserve, repent, God pardon all."[13]

The death and resurrection of Jesus are the cornerstones of the Christian gospel. Having inherited a sinful nature after the fall of Adam, the only salvation for mankind was through grace. Man cannot not sin, as Saint Augustine, the great theologian of the third century has observed. In Libertarian freedom, we are told man makes undetermined choices, and given man's sinful nature, he is saddled with the problem of evil and consequently with sin.

The coming of Jesus was thus to connect man to God, the Father and pay for the sins of mankind through his death. John 3:16 (NAB) is one of the most widely quoted verses from the Bible and has also been called the Gospel in a nutshell: "For God so loved the world that he gave his only Son, so that everyone who believes in him might not perish but might have eternal life."

The Gospel tells us that all who come to Jesus are saved by our debt being nailed to the Cross.

1 Corinthians 15:20-22 (NAB) tells us, "But now Christ has been raised from the dead, the firstfruits of those who have fallen asleep. For since death came through a human being, the resurrection of the dead came also through a human being. For just as in Adam all die, so too in Christ shall all be brought to life."

Finally, let me share the experience of the apostle Paul, who was struck down by lightning on the road to Damascus while pursuing his mission of persecution of the Christians. That was a life-changing event. Paul then went on to preach the gospel of Christ to nations across Europe and became the angel of Christian evangelisation. But in the end, Paul suffered torture, beatings, imprisonment, stoning and finally execution.

Now here's the thing: His letters reveal that Jesus Christ's resurrection was the key to his making sense of his suffering. In his first letter to the Corinthians 15:14-15 (NAB), he says: "And if Christ has not been raised, then empty [too] is our preaching; empty, too, your faith. Then we are also false witnesses to God, because we testified against God that he raised Christ, whom he did not raise if in fact the dead are not raised."

CHAPTER 6

The God Experience in the Time of Covid

In November 2020, as several parts of the world were again tightening regulation screws with stringent lockdowns, the word on the street was a despairing cliché that mourned out loud: "Will this be the new normal?"

By the middle of March 2021, the world had lost well over 2.79 million people to Covid-19 and, according to the World Health Organization (WHO), nearly half of the world's 3.3 billion global workforce were at risk of losing a livelihood, and tens of millions of people are at risk of falling into extreme poverty.

As breadwinners lose jobs, fall ill and die, the food security and nutrition of millions of women, children and men are under threat, with those in low-income countries, particularly the most marginalized populations - small-scale farmers and indigenous peoples – taking the hardest blow.

So, in a statement, WHO said some six months into the pandemic: "Now is the time for global solidarity, especially with the most vulnerable in our societies, particularly in the emerging and developing world. Only together can we overcome the intertwined health and social and economic impacts of the pandemic and prevent its escalation into a protracted humanitarian and food security catastrophe, with the potential loss of already achieved development gains."[1]

The United Nations agencies apparently see it fitting to deliver a secular tone in their statements and therefore propose the view that with global solidarity we can overcome the many ramifications of the pandemic and prevent its escalation into a protracted humanitarian and food security catastrophe.

Indeed, man has to look to science for a vaccine and must heed our scientists on how to speed the process to recovery. But science cannot always unravel the complexities of life working alone. There is a power greater than ourselves, and we only have to open our eyes and look at the stars to make that affirmation.

Covid 19 did bring millions of people to their knees. The churches everywhere had shut their doors in response to directives from their governments. So, we saw people on pavements in several parts of the world bending a knee and with arms stretched supplicating to God for an end to the crisis.

According to PEW Research, large majorities of

Americans who pray daily (86 percent) and U.S. Christians (73 percent) had taken to prayer during the outbreak – but so did some who say they seldom or never pray and people who say they do not belong to any religion (15 percent and 24 percent respectively).[2]

So, is the pandemic God's way of testing his people? Is this a reflection of God's wrath? The passages from scripture, reproduced below might cast a light on that question.

"As he passed by he saw a man blind from birth. His disciples asked him, 'Rabbi, who sinned, this man or his parents, that he was born blind?' Jesus answered, 'Neither he nor his parents sinned; it is so that the works of God might be made visible through him.'" (John 9:1-3, NAB).

In Luke 13:1-5 (NAB), we read:

"At that time some people who were present there told him about the Galileans whose blood Pilate had mingled with the blood of their sacrifices. He said to them in reply, "Do you think that because these Galileans suffered in this way they were greater sinners than all other Galileans? By no means! But I tell you, if you do not repent, you will all perish as they did! Or those eighteen people who were killed when the tower at Siloam fell on them—do you think they were more guilty than everyone else who lived in Jerusalem? By no means! But I tell you, if you do not repent, you will all perish as they did!"

Now, if you turn back the pages of the Old Testament and glean through the story of the ten plagues that challenged the Egyptian Pharaoh at the time of the deliverance of the Jews from slavery, you get a sense of déjà vu.

Pharaoh's notion that he was unassailable, his hubris and his stubborn refusal to present an obsequious response to the demands of God made through Moses, is like a page torn from today's narrative. Pharaoh repeatedly rejected God's demands to set the Hebrews free, contending that he was the oracle and thus brought upon the land the ten plagues.

When Moses and Aaron go up to Pharaoh and declare: "'Thus says the LORD, the God of Israel: Let my people go, that they may hold a feast for me in the wilderness.' Pharaoh answered, 'Who is the LORD, that I should obey him and let Israel go? I do not know the LORD, and I will not let Israel go.'" (Exodus 5:1-2,

NAB)

But, the forty-year trial of the Jews in the wilderness can also be likened to a page torn out of today's narrative.

"Then the LORD said to Moses: I am going to rain down bread from heaven for you. Each day the people are to go out and gather their daily portion; thus will I test them, to see whether they follow my instructions or not.

On the sixth day, however, when they prepare what they bring in, let it be twice as much as they gather on the other days. So Moses and Aaron told all the Israelites, "At evening you will know that it was the LORD who brought you out of the land of Egypt; and in the morning you will see the glory of the LORD, when he hears your grumbling against him. But who are we that you should grumble against us?"

And Moses said, "When the LORD gives you meat to eat in the evening and in the morning your fill of bread, and hears the grumbling you utter against him, who then are we? Your grumbling is not against us, but against the LORD." Then Moses said to Aaron, "Tell the whole Israelite community:

Approach the LORD, for he has heard your grumbling."

But while Aaron was speaking to the whole Israelite community, they turned in the direction of the wilderness, and there the glory of the LORD appeared in the cloud! The LORD said to Moses: 'I have heard the grumbling of the Israelites. Tell them: In the evening twilight you will eat meat, and in the morning you will have your fill of bread, and then you will know that I, the LORD, am your God.'

In the evening, quail came up and covered the camp. In the morning there was a layer of dew all about the camp, and when the layer of dew evaporated, fine flakes were on the surface of the wilderness, fine flakes like hoarfrost on the ground. On seeing it, the Israelites asked one another, "What is this?" for they did not know what it was. But Moses told them, "It is the bread which the LORD has given you to eat. (Exodus 16:4-15, NAB)

The passages confirm that God is not the author of evil. But the call to repent and be saved is the blessed assurance. The pandemic may have been God's way of bringing about change. It's not a reflection of His wrath. He is slow to anger. He is compassionate.

In our arrogance, we fail to see God as the Creator and Sustainer of the universe. The hedonistic doctrine of today's secular society is the fundamental barrier to recognizing the presence of something greater than ourselves.

This moral decline we see has been long since coming with the emergence of a pretentious society. This is really decadence – the tradition of moral uprightness has gradually shifted, expressing itself in progressive thought first and then finally collapsing in the first half of the twentieth century with people, especially in the West embracing a culture of self-emancipation. The Woodstock Rock Festival in 1969 reflected the mood of the era and fed the counter-culture generation that sought to emancipate by casting out restraint, introducing irreverence in a society that was gradually drifting into decadence.

Today, the modern atheist and the average secularist take their cues from scientific theory and some even from scientific imagination. I have read a piece of fiction which proposes how technology can provide a perspective to where we have come from and to where we are going. I have also read a piece of non-fiction which affirms that science will soon put an end to death.

When Stephen Hawking first articulated his ideas about the 'Theory of Everything' in his 1988 book: *A Brief History of Time,* he wrote: "If we do discover a complete theory [of physics], it should in time be understandable in broad principle by everyone. Then we shall all, philosophers, scientists and just ordinary people, be able to take part in the discussion of why it is that we and the universe exist. If we find the answer to that, it would be the ultimate triumph of human reason—for then we would truly know the mind of God."[3]

But as John Cornwell points out in his book *Darwin's Angel,* in 2004, "Stephen Hawking, finally came around to the conclusion that the pursuit of the Theory of Everything was in vain. His decision was a result of revisiting a proof that has fascinated mathematical physicists for many decades."[4]

The dream of a final theory is apparently utopian. It`s time to give God a chance.

Saint Ignatius of Loyola had preached the need to find God in all things. That pursuit is at the core of Ignatian Spirituality. But we ignore that call and instead stand and wonder, "Where is God in all of this."

The testimonies reproduced in this book are stories of great intellectuals and others who had drifted away from God but came back to Him either through a mystical realization of how the fusion of faith and reason can lead to the truth or by a revelation of the fact that without God, life has no purpose.

There is no quick fix for a health crisis that has gripped the planet. A gradual transformation of our societies from hedonism and moral bankruptcy to a mystical realization and the softening of our hearts to witness the presence of God in our lives can pave the way to a state of peace.

At the other end of the spectrum, if we see a God connection in this Covid crisis, then perhaps religion can become an impregnable force working for alleviating poverty and suffering at this difficult time. There is evidence of this work in the countless organizations that address poverty and marginalization.

There are thousands of Christian NGOs across the world engaged in healing the sick, providing for the poor and marginalized, working for social justice. Mother Teresa's work, first in the slums of Calcutta, then through the Missionaries of Charity she founded in 1950, may have touched millions of lives. Her missions are spread across 133 countries, managing homes for people dying of HIV/AIDS, leprosy and tuberculosis and operating soup kitchens, dispensaries and mobile clinics, orphanages and schools.[5]

In much the same way, Bahá'i, Jewish, Muslim, Sikh and other faith groups as well can be seen around the world standing together to effect change.

Several Jewish organizations, especially in the United States, are focussed on fighting social justice and human rights issues. T'ruah brings a rabbinic voice and the power of the Jewish community to protecting and advancing human rights in North America, Israel, and the occupied Palestinian territories.[6]

Canada's Sikh community in Regina is getting national recognition after Prime Minister Justin Trudeau acclaimed its charity work during the COVID-19 pandemic. The Golden Triangle Sikh Association is looking to help international students and isolated seniors by producing packages of vital food ingredients they may not have access to.

The Aga Khan Development Network (AKDN), an endeavour of the Ismaili Imamat to realise the social conscience of Islam, brings together institutions and programs whose combined mandate is to relieve society of ignorance, disease and deprivation. Its primary areas of concern are the poorest regions of Asia and Africa.[7]

So then, why cannot faith groups work for the common good?

There is no quick fix to end the new poverty that

the pandemic has unfolded. But in the face of this temporary crisis, voices of faith can lobby their governments to do more for the poor at this difficult crossroad – even if it means easing the pain of poverty, one person at a time.

Governments across the world must seize the moment and invite the voices of faith that can evolve into a morally-inspired tidal wave to wash away the narrow domestic walls that separate humanity. The voices of faith are probably looking for government leadership to create crisis organization and structure to start the process. The voices of faith come from our societies, and it is from our societies that we are able to reach the poor, the unemployed, the marginalized.

Indeed, COVID 19 has put the world on its head and made us look at life again from another lens. The old is fading away to make room for the new. It has put a break on our way of life. It has taken away our freedom of movement in some measure, as well the freedom to choose. It has reintroduced restraint that we once cast away and is challenging the irreverence, intrinsic in our lifestyles today.

Mankind is turning to science for a saviour. And yet, not all of us trust science. The lurking fear that a vaccine will probably change our DNA was doing the rounds in a rumour mill on social media a couple of months ago. Conspiracy theories have been floating around, inciting fear that the pandemic may be camouflaging a plan to implant trackable microchips via vaccines. There are hideous other claims, although most of them have been debunked.

But be not afraid. Give God a chance. Coming at a time like this, you might want to close your eyes and meditate on Isaiah 35:1-6.

> *The desert and the parched land will be glad; the*
> *   wilderness will rejoice and blossom.*
> *Like the crocus, it will burst into bloom; it will rejoice*
> *   greatly and shout for joy.*
> *The glory of Lebanon will be given to it, the splendor*
> *   of Carmel and Sharon; they will see the glory of*
> *   the LORD, the splendor of our God.*
> *Strengthen the feeble hands, steady the knees that*
> *   give way; say to those with fearful hearts, "Be*
> *   strong, do not fear; your God will come, he will*
> *   come with vengeance; with divine retribution he*
> *   will come to save you."*
> *Then will the eyes of the blind be opened and the ears*
> *   of the deaf unstopped.*
> *Then will the lame leap like a deer, and the mute*
> *   tongue shout for joy.*

*Water will gush forth in the wilderness and streams
in the desert.*

SECTION 2

TESTIMONIES

This second part of the book presents testimonies of famous men and women across the world and other people - spiritually driven individuals who have either felt the healing or saving hand of God in a near-death experience, or in other ways and have reported a sense of having made a conversation with Him. Their testimonies tell about a change of life through a mystical experience, through suffering and death, a new awakening brought about by an abiding faith or through the rigorous search for the purpose of life.

Chapter 1

The Apostle Paul

His conversion to Christianity
ushers in a new morality across Europe

Paul, the brutal persecutor of Jesus' followers, after a conversion on the road to Damascus, is credited with giving Christianity a theology and transforming the shape of the doctrine. He then spread it in his native Cilicia; later with Barnabas, he took it across Antioch in Syria, drawing non-Jewish gentiles to Christ before traveling throughout the eastern Mediterranean up to Greece, setting up churches along the way.

Little is known about Paul's early life. What we know is that he was born in Tarsus in the first decade of the Christian era. Tarsus was the prosperous capital of the Roman Province of Cilicia, now southeastern Turkey. It was where Cleopatra was rowed in her barge like a burnished throne. Saul, as he was called, was the son of a highly religious Jewish family, speaking Aramaic at home and Greek outside. As a youth, he was sent to Jerusalem to become a master of the Law. In conformity with the Talmud, the Jewish code of living, he also learnt a trade, as a tent maker. As an adult, he became one of the most zealous persecutors of the first Christians, who were viewed by the Jewish establishment as heretics or worse.[1]

In his epistle to the Galatians, he says: "For you heard of my former way of life in Judaism, how I persecuted the church of God beyond measure and tried to destroy it, and progressed in Judaism beyond many of my contemporaries among my race, since I was even more a zealot for my ancestral traditions." (Galatians 1:13–14, NAB)

As told in Acts 8:1-2 (NAB), Saul was complicit in the stoning of the first Christian martyr, Stephen. "Now Saul was consenting to his execution. On that day, there broke out a severe persecution of the church in Jerusalem, and all were scattered throughout the countryside of Judea and Samaria, except the apostles. Devout men buried Stephen and made a loud lament over him."

In the Book of Acts, we are told also that Paul was on his way from Jerusalem to Syrian Damascus with a mandate issued by the High Priest to seek out and arrest followers of Jesus, with the intention of returning them to Jerusalem as prisoners for questioning and possible execution. (Acts 9:1-2, NAB) But the journey as he approached Damascus was interrupted when Paul saw a blinding light.

> The men who were traveling with him stood speechless, for they heard the voice but could see no one. Saul got up from the ground, but when he opened his eyes he could see nothing; so they led him by the hand and brought him to Damascus. For three days he was unable to see, and he neither ate nor drank. (Acts 9:7–9, NAB)

The account continues with a description of Ananias of Damascus receiving a divine revelation instructing him to visit Saul at the house of Judas on the Straight Street and ask for a man from Tarsus named Saul and there lay hands on him to restore his sight. Ananias was initially reluctant, having heard about Saul's persecution, but obeyed the divine command.

Then Ananias went to the house and entered it. Placing his hands on Saul, he said, "'Saul, my brother, the Lord has sent me, Jesus who appeared to you on the way by which you came, that you may regain your sight and be filled with the holy Spirit.' Immediately things like scales fell from his eyes and he regained his sight. He got up and was baptized, and when he had eaten, he recovered his strength." (Acts 9:17-19, NAB)

Paul's transformation was profound. After a three-year period of isolation in Arabia, he travelled back to Damascus where he met with Peter and James, the first followers of Jesus, and led the greater part of that early evangelisation. He was both a Jew and a Roman citizen and brought that advantage to bear on his missionary work among both Jewish and Roman populations.

But in the end Paul suffered torture, beatings, imprisonment, stoning and finally execution. His letters reveal that Jesus Christ's resurrection was the key to his making sense of his suffering.

The Christian story had begun shortly after the execution of Jesus with the rapid emergence of belief among his friends and followers that he rose from the dead and was present among them. The first churches were variously organized, though very soon they began to assume a definite hierarchical form to sustain the wildfire spread of the news of the Gospels and the establishment of Christian communities throughout the world.[2]

Christianity swept across the West, bringing a new

morality and influencing the very ethos of European societies across the span of the last 2000 years. The revolutionary teachings of Jesus Christ preached by the apostle Paul brought about a wind of change in Europe, halting infanticide, abolishing slavery, emancipating women, providing the tools to lift up the poor and marginalised, as well as providing for orphans, fostering justice and alleviating the sufferings of mankind.

The Emperor Constantine turned the world upside down by recognizing Christianity instead of persecuting it like his predecessors. It meant freedom of worship and a church building boom. By the end of the 8th century, monasteries could reassemble villages with all their needs met in an enclosure dominated by the abbey church.[3]

Chapter 2

Joseph Pearce

White Supremacist converts to Catholicism while in prison

In 1982, as editor of Bulldog, I was convicted under the Race Relations Act for publishing material 'likely to incite racial hatred' and was sentenced to six months in prison. The trial made national headlines with the result that I spent much of my sentence in isolation and in solitary confinement because the prison authorities were fearful that my presence might provoke trouble between black and white inmates.

"A sound atheist cannot be too careful of the books that he reads." So said C.S. Lewis in his autobiographical apologia, *Surprised by Joy*. These words continue to resonate across the abyss of years that separates me from the abysmal bitterness of my past.

What is true of the atheist is as true of the racist. Looking back into the piteous pits of the hell of hatred that consumed my youth, I can see the role that great Christian writers played in lighting my path out of the darkened depths. Eventually, with their light to guide me, I stumbled out into the dazzling brilliance of Christian day. Looking back along that path, I can see, in my memory's eye, the literary candles that lit the way. There are dozens of candles bearing the name of G.K. Chesterton, of which *Orthodoxy, The Everlasting Man, The Well and the Shallows* and *The Outline of Sanity* shine forth particularly brightly. Almost as many candles bear the name of Chesterton's great friend, Hilaire Belloc, and several bear the name of John Henry Newman. And, of course, there is the flickering presence of Lewis and Tolkien. These and countless others light the path by which I've traveled.

Long before any of these candles were lit, I found myself groping in the unlit tunnel of racial hatred, the angst and anger of which had all but obliterated the blissful memories of a relatively carefree childhood. Guilty of ignorance, I left my innocence behind and advanced into adolescence with the arrogance of pride and prejudice - boyhood bliss blistered by bitterness.

I grew up in a relatively poor neighbourhood in London's East End at a time when large-scale immigration was causing major demographic changes. The influx of large numbers of Indians and Pakistanis was quite literally changing the face of England, darkening the complexion and adding to the complexity of English life. Perhaps inevitably, the arrival of these immigrants caused a great deal of resentment amongst the indigenous population. Racial tensions were high and violence between white and Asian youths was becoming commonplace. It was in this highly charged atmosphere that I emerged into angry adolescence.

At the age of fifteen, I joined the National Front, a new force in British politics which demanded the compulsory repatriation of all non-white immigrants. As a political activist, my life revolved around street demonstrations, many of which became violent. I filled my empty head and inflamed my impassioned heart with racist ideology and elitist philosophy. It was at this time that I made what I now consider to be my Faustian pact, i.e., my pact with the Devil; not that I had heard of Faust nor, as an agnostic, did I have any particular belief in the Devil. Nonetheless, I recall making a conscious 'wish' that I would give everything if I could work full-time for the National Front. My 'wish' was granted, and I abandoned my education to devote myself wholeheartedly to becoming a full-time 'racial revolutionary'.

I never looked back. At the age of sixteen, I became

editor of *Bulldog*, the newspaper of the Young National Front, and, three years later, became the editor of *Nationalism Today*, a 'higher brow' ideological journal. At eighteen, I became the youngest member of the party's governing body. Whether I believed in him or not, the Devil had certainly been diligent in answering my 'wish.'

Apart from the racism, the sphere of my bitterness also included a disdain for Catholicism, partly because the terrorists of the IRA were Catholics and partly because I had imbibed the anti-Catholic prejudice of many Englishmen that Catholicism is a 'foreign' religion. Such prejudice is deeply rooted in the national psyche, stretching back to the anti-Catholicism of Henry VIII and his English Reformation, to Elizabeth I and the Spanish Armada, to James I and the Gunpowder Plot, and to William of Orange and the so-called 'Glorious' Revolution. I knew enough of English history – or, at least, enough of the prejudiced Protestant view of it that I had imbibed in my ignorance – to see Catholicism as an enemy to the Nationhood which, as a racial nationalist, I now espoused with a quasi-religious fervour.

It was, however, in the context of 'the Troubles' in Northern Ireland that my anti-Catholicism would reveal itself in its full ugliness. The IRA's bombing campaign was at its height during the 1970s, and my hatred of Republican terrorism led to my becoming involved in the volatile politics of Ulster. I joined the Orange Order, a pseudo-masonic secret society whose sole purpose of existence is to oppose 'popery,' i.e., Catholicism. Technically, although only 'Protestants' were allowed to join the Orange Order, any actual belief in God did not appear necessary. As a 'Protestant' agnostic, I was allowed to join, and a friend of mine, an avowed atheist, was also accepted without qualms. Ultimately, the only qualification was not a love for Christ but a hatred of the Church.

In October 1978, still only seventeen, I flew to Derry in Northern Ireland to assist in the organization of a National Front march. Tensions were high in the city, and, towards the end of the day, riots broke out between the Protestant demonstrators and the police. For the duration of the evening and well into the night, petrol bombs were thrown at the police, Catholic homes were attacked and Catholic-owned shops were looted and destroyed. I had experienced political violence on the streets of England but nothing on the sheer scale of the anger and violence that I experienced in Northern Ireland.

My appetite whetted, I became further embroiled

in the politics of Ulster, forging friendships and political alliances with the leaders of the Protestant paramilitary groups, the Ulster Volunteer Force (UVF) and the Ulster Defence Association (UDA). During a secret meeting with the army council of the UVF, it was suggested that I use my connections with extremist groups in other parts of the world to open channels for arms smuggling. On another occasion, an 'active service unit' of the UVF, i.e. a terrorist cell, offered their 'services' to me, assuring me of their willingness to assassinate any 'targets' that I would like 'taken out' and expressing their eagerness to show me their arsenal of weaponry as a mark of their 'good faith'. I declined their offer, as politely as possible – one does not wish to offend 'friends' such as these! They were dangerous times. Within a few years, two of my friends in Northern Ireland had been murdered by the IRA.

Back in England, violence continued to erupt at National Front demonstrations. Outside an election meeting in an Indian area of London in 1979, at which I was one of the speakers, a riot ensued in which one demonstrator was killed. A few years later, a friend of mine, an elderly man, was killed at another election meeting, though on that occasion I was not present.

Predictably, perhaps, it was only a matter of time before my extremist politics brought me into conflict with the law. In 1982, as editor of *Bulldog*, I was convicted under the Race Relations Act for publishing material 'likely to incite racial hatred' and was sentenced to six months in prison. The trial made national headlines with the result that I spent much of my sentence in isolation and in solitary confinement because the prison authorities were fearful that my presence might provoke trouble between black and white inmates. Ironically, one of the other prisoners in the top security wing was an IRA sympathizer who had been imprisoned for slashing a portrait of Princess Diana with a knife. He and I saw ourselves as 'political prisoners,' not as mere 'common criminals,' like the murderers, serving life sentences, who constituted the majority of the other prisoners on the top security wing.

Unrepentant, I continued to edit *Bulldog* following my release and was duly charged once again with offences under the Race Relations Act. On the second occasion, I was sentenced to twelve months imprisonment. Thus, I spent both my twenty-first and twenty-fifth birthdays behind bars.

During the first of my prison sentences, Auberon Waugh, a well-known writer and son of the great Catholic novelist, Evelyn Waugh, had referred to me as a 'wretched youth'. How right he was! Wretched and wrecked upon the rock of my own hardness of heart. Years later, when asked by the priest who was instructing me in the Catholic faith to write an essay on my conversion, I began it with the opening lines of John Newton's famous hymn extolling the 'amazing grace ... that saved a wretch like me'. Even today, when forced to look candidly into the blackness of my past, I am utterly astonished at the truly amazing grace that somehow managed to take root in the desert of my soul.

How then did the cactus of grace, growing at first unheeded in the desert of my just deserts, become the cataract of life-giving waters washing my sins away in the sacramental grace of confession? How, to put the matter more bluntly and blandly, was I freed from the prison of my sinful convictions? How was I brought from the locked door of my prison cell to the open arms of Mother Church?

With the wisdom of hindsight, I perceive that the seeds of my future conversion were planted as early as 1980 when I was still only nineteen years old. In what barren soil they were planted! At the time, I was at the very height, or depth, of my political fanaticism and was indulging the worst excesses of my anti-Catholic prejudices in the dirty waters of Ulster Protestantism.

Few could have been further from St Peter's Gate than I.

The seeds were planted in the genuine desire to seek a political and economic alternative to the sins of communism and the cynicism of consumerism. During the confrontations on the streets with my Marxist opponents, I was incensed by their suggestion that, as an anti-communist, I was, ipso facto, a 'storm-trooper of capitalism'. I refused to believe that the only alternative to Mammon was Marx. I was convinced that communism was a red herring and that it was possible to have a socially just society without social-ism.

In my quest to discover such an alternative, some-one suggested that I read more about the distributist ideas of Belloc and Chesterton. At this juncture, one hears echoes once again of Lewis's stricture that 'a sound atheist cannot be too careful of the books that he reads,' not least because the book to which he was specifically referring was Chesterton's *The Everlasting Man*, a book which would precipitate Lewis's first tentative steps to conversion. In this, at least, I can claim a real parallel between C.S. Lewis and myself. For me, as for him, a book by Chesterton would lead towards conversion. In my case, however, the book which was destined to have such a profound influence was a lesser known book of Chesterton's.

The friend who suggested that I study the distributist ideas of Chesterton informed me that I should buy his book *The Outline of Sanity*, but also that I should read an invaluable essay on the subject, entitled 'Reflections on a Rotten Apple,' which was to be found in a collection of his essays entitled *The Well and the Shallows*. As he suggested, I purchased these two books and sat down expectantly to read the volume of essays. Imagine my surprise, and my consternation, to discover that the book was, for the most part, a defence of the Catholic faith against various modern attacks upon it. And imagine my confusion when I discovered that I could not fault Chesterton's logic.

The wit and wisdom of Chesterton had pulled the rug out from under my smug prejudices against the Catholic Church. From that moment, I began to discover Her as She is, and not as She is alleged to be by Her enemies. I began the journey from the rumour that She was the Whore of Babylon to the realization that She was in fact the Bride of Christ.

It was, however, destined to be a long journey. I was lost in Dante's dark wood, so deeply lost that I had perhaps already strayed into the Inferno. It is a long and arduous climb from there to the foot of Mount

Purgatory. I was, however, in good company. If Dante had Virgil, I had Chesterton. He would accompany me faithfully every inch of the way, present always through the pages of his books. I began to devour everything by Chesterton that I could get my hands on, consuming his words with ravenous delight. Through Chesterton, I came to know Belloc; then Lewis; then Newman. During the second prison sentence, I first read *The Lord of the Rings* and, though I did not at that time fathom the full mystical depths of the Catholicism in Tolkien's myth, I was aware of its goodness, its objective morality and the well of virtue from which it drew. And, of course, I was aware that Tolkien, like Chesterton, Belloc and Newman, was a Catholic. Why was it that most of my favourite writers were Catholics?

It was during the second prison sentence that I first started to consider myself a Catholic. When, as is standard procedure, I was asked my religion by the prison authorities at the beginning of my sentence, I announced that I was a Catholic. I wasn't, of course, at least not technically, but it was my first affirmation of faith, even to myself. A significant landmark had been reached.

Another significant landmark during the second prison sentence was my first fumbling efforts at prayer.

I am not aware of ever having prayed prior to my arrival at Wormwood Scrubs prison in December 1985, at least not if one discounts the schoolboy prayers recited parrot-fashion to an unknown and unlooked-for God many years earlier during drab and lukewarm school services. Now, in the desolation of my cell, I fumbled my fingers over the beads of a Rosary that someone had sent me. I had no idea how to say it. I did not know the Hail Mary or the Glory Be, and I could not remember the Lord's Prayer. Nonetheless, I ad-libbed my way from bead to bead, uttering prayers of my own devising, pleading from the depths of my piteous predicament for the faith, hope and love that my mind and heart desired. It was a start, small but significant.

My release from prison in 1986 heralded the beginning of the end of my life as a political extremist. Increasingly disillusioned, I extricated myself from the organisation which had been my life, and which had delineated my very raison d'etre, for more than a decade. As a fifteen-year-old, I had 'wished' to give my life to the 'cause,' now, in my mid-twenties, I desired only to give my life to Christ. If the Devil had taken my earlier 'wish' and had granted it infernally, Christ would take my new-found desire and grant it purga-torially. Having spent the whole of the 1980s in a spiritual arm-wrestle, fought within my heart and my head between the hell of hatred within myself and the well of love promised and poured out by Christ, I finally 'came home' to the loving embrace of Holy Mother Church on the Feast of St Joseph, 1989. Today, I still find myself utterly amazed at the grace that could save a wretch like me.

Chapter 3

C.S. Lewis

His conversion inspired many to come out of that trap in which most atheists land up

C.S. Lewis has been an inspiration to several people seeking to be extricated from the trap in which most atheists ultimately land up. Among them are the eminent Dr. Francis Collins, the director of the National Institutes of Health (NIH) and chief of the Human Genome Project.

Clive Staples (C.S.) Lewis (1898–1963) was a British writer and lay theologian. He held academic positions in English literature at both Oxford and Cambridge University and is best known for his works of fiction, especially *The Screwtape Letters*, *The Chronicles of Narnia*, and *The Space Trilogy*, as well as for his non-fiction Christian apologetics: *Mere Christianity*, *Miracles*, and *The Problem of Pain*.

Lewis was raised in an Anglican family and, according to his 1955 memoir *Surprised by Joy*, abandoned his faith during adolescence, when he would sometimes despair about the non-existence of God and paradoxically quote the Roman poet Titus Lucretius to defend his argument for atheism.[1] Lucretius is reported to have said: "*Had God designed the world, it would not be a world so frail and faulty as we see.*"

Lewis's interest in the works of George MacDonald and G.K. Chesterton's *The Eternal Man* were part of what turned him away from his impregnable atheist position. MacDonald was a Scottish author, poet and Christian Minister, who wrote several works of Christian theology. Lewis's discovery of MacDonald`s book *Phantastes* was particularly influential. As he wrote later in his preface to *George MacDonald: An Anthology:* "Phantastes.... had about it a sort of cool, morning innocence...what it actually did to me was to convert, even to baptise my imagination."[2]

But it was Tolkien's friendship that brought him to the encounter with Christ after an after-dinner stroll in the grounds of Magdalen college, discussing ancient myths. Lewis, of course, had vigorously resisted conversion at first, noting that he was brought into Christianity like a prodigal.

His faith profoundly affected his work, and his

wartime radio broadcasts on the subject of Christianity brought him wide acclaim.

I have read Lewis's book *Mere Christianity* with great interest and one of the passages in that book that struck me as being deeply profound is his response to the question: Who is Jesus? This is what he says:

> "I am trying here to prevent anyone saying the really foolish thing that people often say about Jesus: I'm ready to accept Jesus as a great moral teacher, but I don't accept his claim to be God. That is the one thing we must not say. A man who was merely a man and said the sort of things Jesus said would not be a great moral teacher. He would either be a lunatic — on the level with the man who says he is a poached egg — or else he would be the Devil of Hell. You must make your choice. Either this man was, and is, the Son of God, or else a madman or something worse. You can shut him up for a fool, you can spit at him and kill him as a demon or you can fall at his feet and call him Lord and God, but let us not come with any patronising nonsense about his being a great human teacher. He has not left that open to us. He did not intend to."[3]

C.S. Lewis has been an inspiration to several people seeking to be extricated from the trap in which most atheists ultimately land up. Among them are people like Dr. Francis Collins, the director of the National Institutes of Health (NIH) and chief of the Human Genome Project. Collins is an American geneticist known for his landmark discoveries of disease genes.

When he was at a loss seeking God, he talked to a pastor one day who just handed him a book by C.S. Lewis that swept him off his feet. In a video presentation on BioLogos he says: "In the first two or three pages, I realized that my arguments against faith were really those of a school boy... I had imagined that faith and reason were at opposite poles. And here was this deep intellectual who was convincing me quickly page by page that reason and faith go hand in hand."[4]

In his book *Mere Christianity*, this is what Lewis says about the Moral Law:

"Supposing you hear a cry for help from a man in danger, you will probably feel two desires – one a desire to give help (due to your herd instinct), the other a desire to keep out of danger. But you will find inside you, in addition to the two impulses, a third thing which tells you that you ought to follow the impulse to help and suppress the impulse to run away. Now this thing that judges between two in-stincts...cannot itself be either of them. The moral Law tells us the tune we have to play; our instincts are merely the keys."[5]

Then, on the evidence of God, this is what Lewis says in *Mere Christianity*:

"If there was a controlling power outside the uni-verse, it could not show itself to us as one of the facts inside the universe - no more than the architect of a house could actually be a wall or staircase or fireplace in that house. The only way in which we could expect it to show itself would be inside ourselves as an influence or a command try-ing to get us to behave in a certain way. And that is just what we do find inside ourselves."[6]

Chapter 4

Scientist Francis Collins

Doctor, what do you believe?

"The universe had a beginning - as virtually all scientists are coming to the conclusion - about 13.7 billion years ago in an unimaginable singularity when the universe, smaller than a golf ball, suddenly appeared and then began flying apart and has been flying apart ever since. We can calculate that singularity by noticing just how far those galaxies are receding from us as well as things like the background microwave radiation echo of the Big Bang. But, of course, our science cannot look back beyond that point and so it seems that something came out of nothing. Well, nature isn't supposed to allow that. So if nature is not able to create itself, how did the universe get here?"

Dr. Francis Collins is an American physician and geneticist noted for his landmark discoveries of disease genes and his administration of the Human Genome

Project whose goal was to map and understand the code of life. He is also author of the book *The Language of God.* But going back in time, in his presentation to the 2019 BioLogos Conference, he tells of how by the time he was in graduate school he had drifted toward atheist thinking. The title of his presentation: *Doctor, What Do You Believe?*

In that presentation, Dr. Collins narrates a conversation with a wonderful elderly woman – a patient who knew her life was coming to a close and told him in a very simple way about her faith. When she was done with her narrative, she turned to him and said: "Doctor, what do you believe?" Dr. Collins says he had never been asked that question before... and he realized then that he did not know the answer. "I had made a decision that there was no God and I really never thought of looking at the evidence..."

So, at a loss, some days later he sought the help of a church minister who lived down the road from him on Chapel Road, North Carolina. The pastor apparently listened keenly to his questions and then handed him a book by Oxford scholar C.S. Lewis.

Dr. Collins took the book home and began to read. "In the first two or three pages, I realized that my arguments against faith were really those of a school boy... I had imagined that faith and reason were at opposite poles. And here was this deep intellectual who was convincing me quickly, page by page, that reason and faith go hand in hand."

Now, in his presentation at the 2019 BioLogos (Science and Faith) conference, Dr. Collins lists some of the pointers to God which nature provides:

1. There is something instead of nothing.
2. The unreasonable effectiveness of mathematics
3. The Big Bang
4. The precise tuning of physical constants in the universe
5. The Moral Law

Let me quote Dr. Collins' on his observations of the first, third and fourth pointers:

"Here's one that seems like an obvious statement, but maybe it's not so obvious," he says: "There is something instead of nothing. No reason that should be."

There is the Big Bang: "The fact that the universe had a beginning - as virtually all scientists are coming to the conclusion - about 13.7 billion years ago in an unimaginable singularity when the universe, smaller than a golf ball, suddenly appeared and then began flying apart and has been flying apart ever since. We can calculate that singularity by noticing just how far those galaxies are receding from us and things like the background microwave radiation echo of the Big Bang. But, of course, our science cannot look back beyond that point and so it seems that something came out of nothing. Well, nature isn't supposed to allow that. So if nature is not able to create itself, how did the universe get here? You can't postulate that it was created by some natural force because then (the question is) what created that natural force. So the only plausible – it seems to me - explanation, is that there must be a supernatural force..."

Dr. Collins contends that would be God who is not bound by space nor time. In his book *The Language of God*, he observes with a tone of despair: "The Big Bang calls for a divine explanation."

He then goes on to speak of the wonder of the physical constants which are believed to hold around the universe, finely tuned in a way that if they were slightly different, the universe would probably be unfriendly to life. Setting his scientific arguments like ducks in a row, he makes a marvellous case for how reason can take you to the point where you see that God is very real.

Dr. Collins ends then with the realization that God's holiness can reconcile with our sinfulness "....only through the person of Jesus Christ who not only claimed to know God but to be God and who in this uplifting, sacrificial act died on the cross and then rose from the dead to provide this bridge between my imperfections and God's holiness in a way that made more sense than I ever dreamed it could."

In conclusion, he says: "So on a wonderful summer morning, in the dewy grass of the Cascade mountains in the northwest, I fell on my knees and I said: 'I get it. I am yours. I want to be your follower from now until eternity.' That was forty-one years ago."

Chapter 5

Horatio Spafford

Personal troubles rivalled
the miseries of Job in the Old Testament

A chain of tragedies failed to shake Horatio's faith in God. He set off at once to be reunited with his wife. Then a couple of days into the voyage, as he contemplated alone in his cabin, the captain summoned him to the bridge of the vessel. Then pointing to his charts, he is reported to have shown Horatio the very spot where the Ville du Havre had sunk, and where his daughters had perished.

It was the best of times. It was the worst of times. Those are the famous opening lines of *A Tale of Two Cities* by the English novelist Dickens and they somehow ring true for the life and times of Horatio Gates Spafford, a wealthy American who, although he was born in New York (20 October 1828), built his estate in

Chicago. A devout Christian, Horatio, and his wife, Anna, actively engaged in Christian apostolic work and opened their doors to a host of friends, among whom was the world-famous evangelist, Dwight L. Moody.

The Spaffords were blessed with five kids and of course with a wealthy estate - his investments made in blue chip properties in the home city. Horatio was a top-ranking lawyer. Those were the best of times.

But then came a twist in the tale. A first tragedy hit and on its heels a chain of devastations. Horatio and Anna lost their four-year-old son, Horatio Jr., to scarlet fever. Then the following year, October 1871, the Great Chicago fire broke out in or around a barn on the city's southwest side and the raging flames swallowed up an estimated 300 lives and left 100,000 others homeless. According to reports, more than 17,000 structures were destroyed, and damages were estimated at $200 million.[1] Horatio's blue-chip properties crumbled, and its embers lay burning in dying fires. In the midst of burning flames and despite their colossal financial losses, the Spaffords engaged in comforting the grief stricken and bringing comfort to those in great need, to demonstrate the love of Christ.

Spafford's troubles have been likened to the miseries of Job in the Old Testament - a prosperous man who was beset by horrendous disasters which took away all that he held dear. He struggled to understand why God had cast him into this conundrum of evil but held fast to his loyalty to God. Job's declaration, "I know that my redeemer liveth" (Job 19:25), is considered by some Christians to be a proto-Christian reference to Christ as the Redeemer. In the end, the Lord restored the fortunes of Job and gave him two-fold of what he lost. (Job 42:10)

The worst of times were not over for the Spaffords with the Great Chicago Fire. Two years later, in 1873, Horatio worked out a plan for a family holiday in England that coincided with his friend, evangelist D. L. Moody's preaching season in the autumn. All was well, until before the final moment of departure on a steamship. Horatio was pressured to stay back because of urgent business. So, he sent his family ahead: his wife Anna and their four remaining children, all daughters, Annie, Margaret Lee, Elizabeth, and Tanetta.

On 21 November 1873, while crossing the Atlantic on that steamship, Ville du Havre, their vessel was struck by an iron sailing ship. The devastation was horrific: 226 people lost their lives as the Ville du Havre sank within only twelve minutes. All four of Horatio Spafford's daughters perished. Anna Spafford, however, remarkably survived. She was found in an unconscious state, floating on a raft. With rescue teams, she subsequently arrived in Cardiff, South Wales, where upon arrival, Anna despatched a telegram to her husband with those poignant words: "Saved alone...."[2]

The chain of tragedies, anyway, failed to shake Horatio's faith in God. He set off at once to be reunited with his wife. Then a couple of days into the voyage, as he contemplated alone in his cabin, the captain summoned him to the bridge of the vessel. Then pointing to his charts, he is reported to have shown Horatio the very spot where the Ville du Havre had sunk and where his daughters had perished. It is said that Spafford returned to his cabin soon after and wrote the lines: *"It is well with my soul,"* which is now a well-remembered hymn sung by Christians around the world. These are the first four lines:

"When peace like a river, attendeth my way.
When sorrows like sea billows roll
Whatever my lot, thou hast taught me to say
It is well, it is well with my soul."

But the worst of times were yet not over for the Spaffords, who upon returning to America began life anew, while seeking to understand, some day, God's purpose in their lives. Anna gave birth to three more children, but the Spaffords were hit with one more tragedy. On February 11, 1880, their only son, Horatio Jr. - named after his older brother who had passed away - also died at the age of four.[3]

In August 1881, the Spaffords went to Jerusalem as a party of thirteen adults and three children to set up an American Colony. Colony members, joined by Swedish Christians, engaged in philanthropic work among the people of Jerusalem regardless of their religious affiliation, gaining the trust of the local Muslim, Jewish and Christian communities.[4]

There they lived out the gospel of Jesus: "For I was hungry and you gave me food, I was thirsty and you gave me drink, a stranger and you welcomed me, naked and you clothed me, ill and you cared for me, in prison and you visited me." (Matthew 25:35-36, NAB)

Horatio Spafford is reported to have died of malaria on 16 October 1888. Anna went on to work in the surrounding areas of Jerusalem until her own death on April 17, 1923.

Chapter 6

John Newton

A former slaver turned preacher

In 1750, he made a further voyage as master of the slave ship 'Duke of Argyle' and two voyages on the 'African'. He admitted that he was a ruthless business-man and an unfeeling observer of the Africans he traded. Slave revolts on board ship were frequent. Newton mounted guns and muskets on the desk aimed at the slaves' quarters. Slaves were lashed and put in thumb-screws to keep them quiet.

John Newton (1725-1807) was an Anglican clergy-man and former slave ship master. It took him a long time to speak out against the Slave Trade, but he had an influence on many young evangelical Christians, particularly William Wilberforce.

At just eleven years old, Newton went to sea with his father. In 1743, he was on his way to a position as a slave master on a plantation in Jamaica when he was pressed into naval service. He became a midshipman, but after demotion for trying to desert, he requested an exchange to a slave ship bound for West Africa.

Eventually, he reached the coast of Sierra Leone, where he became the servant of an abusive slave trader. In 1748, he was rescued by a sea captain and returned to England. During a storm, when it was thought the ship might sink, he prayed for deliverance. This experience began his conversion to evangelical Christianity. Later, whilst aboard a slave vessel bound for the West Indies, he became ill with a violent fever and asked for God's mercy; an experience he claimed was the turning point in his life.

Despite this, he continued to participate in the Slave Trade. In 1750, he made a further voyage as master of the slave ship 'Duke of Argyle' and two voyages on the 'African'. He admitted that he was a ruthless businessman and an unfeeling observer of the Africans he traded. Slave revolts on board ship were frequent. Newton mounted guns and muskets on the desk aimed at the slaves' quarters. Slaves were lashed and put in thumbscrews to keep them quiet.

In 1754, after a serious illness, he gave up seafaring altogether. In 1757, he applied for the Anglican priesthood. It was seven years before he was accepted. On

17th June 1764, he finally became a priest at Olney in Buckinghamshire. He became well-known for his pastoral care and respected by both Anglicans and non-conformists.

He collaborated with William Cowper to produce a volume of hymns, including 'Amazing Grace'. So popular was his preaching, that the church could not accommodate all those who flocked to hear him. Newton began to deeply regret his involvement in the Slave Trade. After he became Rector of St Mary Woolnoth, in London in 1779, his advice was sought by many influential figures in Georgian society, among them the young M.P., William Wilberforce. Wilberforce was contemplating leaving politics for the ministry. But Newton encouraged him to stay in Parliament and "serve God where he was". Wilberforce took his advice and spent the rest of his life working towards the abolition of slavery.

In 1787, Newton wrote a tract supporting the campaign, 'Thoughts upon the African Slave Trade,' which was very influential. It graphically described the horrors of the Slave Trade and his role in it. He later joined William Wilberforce in the campaign for abolition of the Slave Trade. In February 1807, when the act to abolish the Slave Trade finally became law,

John Newton, nearly blind and near death, "rejoiced to hear the wonderful news."

Chapter 7

Dr. Kevin Vost

St. Thomas allowed me to make the leap of faith without jumping away from reason

An old saying goes, "a little philosophy leads to atheism," and by age 18, Dr. Vost had been so led. He says: "I immersed myself in the writings of Voltaire, Nietzsche (complete with his own, yet quite different, conception of the "superman"), of Bertrand Russell, and especially of Ayn Rand, since she described her philosophy of Objectivism as the natural outgrowth of Aristotle's writings. All of them (excepting Aristotle) viewed the idea of God as unreasonable and unnecessary, and at that point in my life, reason became my god."

What does it mean to be a man? What is the key to happiness and fulfillment? I've always thought the ancient Greek philosophers were really onto something with their answer — the complete and happy man has *a sound mind in a sound body.*

Before I knew about those Greeks, my childhood embodiment of such a man came straight from my television set. Here was a man more powerful than a speeding locomotive and able to leap tall buildings in a single bound, yet totally devoted to "Truth, Justice, and the American Way." My early childhood fascination with Superman, you see, led me later to the Man of Steel's ancient Greek prototypes — to Odysseus and Achilles, and most especially, to the mighty Hercules himself.

Now there was a model for a sound body — a mental image to fuel my fires as I prepared for bodybuilding and power lifting competitions in my teens. And as far as the mind goes, I discovered Aristotle, the Father of Logic, around that time. Social scientist Charles Murray, in his book *Human Accomplishment,* ranks Aristotle as *numero uno* in overall human achievement! It seemed I had found my ultimate model for excellence of mind.

By my teens, I'm pretty much set in my ways with my models for manhood and happiness, but for a brief foray into intense Christianity. When I was about fifteen and had started giving my abstract thinking abilities a little exercise, it occurred to me that *if the lessons of my Christian (Roman Catholic) upbringing were true, then nothing in the universe was more important,* and it was time to truly start living by the faith.

I was raised Catholic after all. We went to Mass every Sunday, and my brother and sister and I had always gone to Catholic schools. We were taught by wonderful Dominican sisters. I hesitate to admit that we often called them "penguins" because of their long black-and-white habits since I have in later times grown so impressed by the religious who openly wear their devotion to Christ "on their sleeves" — and everywhere else. From those early years at home and school, I gleaned a strong sense of morality, of right and wrong, and a respect for the intellect and self-discipline.

Still, I cannot say that I learned a great deal about the particulars of the Catholic Faith. At home, we really didn't talk much at all about Christ or the Church. As I have mentioned, though, at around age 15, I had somewhat of a conversion experience, triggered by that intellectual "Aha!" regarding the ultimate importance of Christ.

My only really devout Christian friends at that time were not Catholic, though. One had converted away from Catholicism, but most had long been members of one or two local non-denominational or Pentecostal churches. I attended services with them with some profit. Many of these people's lives had been turned around by their devotion to Christ. Some, I found, did not consider Catholics true Christians, but even in my state of relative ignorance of my own faith, I realized that we had Christ, too, and I did not abandon Catholicism for any form of separated Christianity. No, I ran into trouble elsewhere — within the musty pages of old philosophy books.

Always a bit of a bookworm, my reading took me deeper into philosophy. An old saying goes, *"a little philosophy leads to atheism,"* and by age 18 I had been so led. I immersed myself in the writings of Voltaire, Nietzsche (complete with his own, yet quite different, conception of the "superman"), of Bertrand Russell, and especially of Ayn Rand, since she described her philosophy of Objectivism as the natural outgrowth of Aristotle's writings. All of them (excepting Aristotle) viewed the idea of God as unreasonable and unnecessary, and at that point in my life, reason became my god.

As the years went by, my "little bit" of philosophy developed into 20 years of study, and I assumed that old maxim could not apply to me. Still, I could not completely forget my nostalgic feelings for my Catholic upbringing. My lovely wife, Kathy, and I sent our children to Catholic schools. (I could rationalize that Thomas Jefferson, another of my idols, had sent his daughters to be taught by Jesuits in France.)

Personally, I deeply wanted to believe, but I did not feel that in good conscience I could pretend to believe what I did not. I remember reading philosopher Mortimer Adler's *How to Think About God* twice, years apart, hoping this would allow me to go there, but it did not quite bring me home.

Then, at age 43, along came a 13th-century Dominican friar by the name of St. Thomas Aquinas, and he turned everything upside down — or maybe I should say, right side up!

When Charles Darwin first encountered the biological writings of Aristotle, he described modern scientific giants of his day as "mere schoolboys compared to old Aristotle." So, too, when I discovered the firsthand writings of St. Thomas Aquinas, I discovered that the modern philosophers I had been following were *"mere schoolboys (and a schoolgirl)"* compared to old St. Thomas Aquinas!

St. Thomas showed me how faith and reason need not be in opposition, and that *a person who thinks can also be a person who believes.* What a liberation! Here was a true-to-life *Superman of the Mind* who loved God with all his heart and soul.

I found out not long afterwards that Pope Leo XIII,

in his encyclical *Aeterni Patris* of 1879, had written about "those, who with minds alienated from the faith … claim reason as their sole mistress and guide." Further, he noted that "apart from the supernatural help of God, nothing is better calculated to heal those minds and bring them into favor with the Catholic faith" than the writings of the Church Fathers and Scholastic philosophers — St. Thomas being their greatest exemplar.

St. Thomas Aquinas was then the great hope for the conversion of modern intellectuals devoted to reason. Boy, did Pope Leo have my number, so many years before I was born!

St. Thomas allowed me to make the leap of faith without jumping away from reason. He, too, admired the Greeks, and he knew Aristotle exceedingly well. Some claim it is easier to grasp Aristotle's philosophy by reading Aquinas than by reading Aristotle himself. St. Thomas did not merely throw Aristotle's name around in passing, but he wrote complete commentaries on every single line of many of Aristotle's books, and he peerlessly integrated logic and rational philosophy with Christian revelation in his masterful *Summa Theologica.*

There is only one truth, wrote St. Thomas. Reason and Revelation are not contradictory. Faith does not contradict reason, but it takes us farther and higher than our reason can go, serving, as Pope Saint John Paul II would write in his 1998 encyclical *Fides et Ratio* (Faith and Reason), as the two wings on which we rise to the truth.

St. Thomas's writings were a real revelation to me. Little did I know that more than 700 years ago he had so soundly answered all the arguments of the atheists, who to this day proclaim that the idea of God is self-contradictory or completely unnecessary to explain the universe.

His writings brought me back to Christ and His Church. The next thing I knew, we were back at Mass, and I began making up for a quarter of a century of lost time by devouring the New Testament and everything I could find by and about St. Thomas, St. Augustine, G.K. Chesterton, C.S. Lewis, and others. EWTN became my television fare, and *The Journey Home* my every Monday ritual. My family and I even wound up in Rome with a group from our parish during the week of Pope John Paul II's funeral in April of 2005.

Admittedly, my story is a bit unusual in our time, although I have encountered a few folks since I've been back who were also drawn back by St. Thomas's writings. Typically today, threats to Christianity come not so much from abstract philosophies as from distortions popularized in modern books and movies made for mass consumption. "Didn't you know," a co-worker asks, "that Jesus and Mary Magdalene were married and had a child?" "It was Constantine, after all, who wrote the New Testament and came up with the idea that Jesus was God," proclaims another. And a third informs me that the Church suppressed the Gnostic Gospels, like the *Gospel of Thomas,* which tells the "true story" with a much more pro-feminist message.

Interesting pronouncements, but I seem to recall from a little green book on my library shelf *(An Exhortation to the Greeks)* that Clement of Alexandria, who died before Constantine was born, was one of the many early Church Fathers who regularly spoke of Jesus as God. No marriage or children of Jesus are mentioned in any of the four Gospels. And wasn't that *Gospel of Thomas* actually a bit negative in its stance on women, stating that women must become males to be worthy of the kingdom of heaven?

Personally, I was also wowed to see how God had used my twenty-five years in the atheistic wilderness to prepare me for my return to the Church and even to help me acquire skills that my formal training in psychology and avocation of philosophy help to do my own share to spread the wisdom of St. Thomas Aquinas with popular readers today.

Sometimes, St. Thomas' relevance came through in the most surprising of ways. For example, one of my own specialty areas in psychology was memory. My master's thesis examined memory improvement in adolescents through the use of particular memory strategies, and my doctoral dissertation examined the loss of memory and other higher intellectual capacities that accompanies dementia toward the end of life.

You can imagine my amazement, upon my return to the Church, when I recalled that St. Thomas had been called "the patron saint" of memory-aiding techniques by a secular historian! (See *Summa Theologica,* II-II, Question 49, article 1 and his *Commentary on Aristotle's On Memory and Recollection* for examples of the reason behind this.)

In turn, this discovery led to my current avocation of writing books about St. Thomas's approach to memory, and then the virtues, the seven deadly sins, the seven gifts of the Holy Spirit, and more (working now on a book about thinking like Aquinas). The Holy Spirit's blessings have just kept pouring out to me and my family through the writings of St. Thomas Aquinas.

It seems to me that the most prevalent threat to Christianity today is not so much exposure to the bad philosophy of the godless philosophers as it is a lack of knowledge of the contents and history of one's own faith — a knowledge that will not fall prey to popular distortions of Church history and a faith that can inoculate one from the bite of bad philosophy and heal those already bitten.

I hope and pray that all Catholics will come to know and love Christ and His Church so well that they will never be led astray by bad philosophy or popular media. If such education is not supplied in their formal schooling, they can obtain it through study of the *Catechism of the Catholic Church,* through immersion in Catholic media like radio, television, and books, and for kindred souls, through the writings of St. Thomas and his popularizers.

As for me, St. Thomas Aquinas, the philosopher of God, saved me from the godless philosophers by applying the remedy of both faith and reason. I've felt thankful to God ever since.

Kevin Vost, Psy.D., has taught psychology at the University of Illinois at Springfield and Aquinas College in Nashville, Tennessee. An author of 15 books, including **Memorize the Faith!** *and* **The Catholic Guide to Loneliness,** *Dr. Vost lives with his wife, Kathy, in Springfield, IL. His website is www.drvost.com.*

Chapter 8

Teresa Arthur

"Someone touched me"

That day the rug was pulled from right under my feet. The radiologists examined all those tests results and then handed over a verdict to the doctor I was consulting. She came into the ward very disturbed. "I'm afraid, it's not good news," she said. "They see cancer."

"And a woman afflicted with hemorrhages for twelve years, who [had spent her whole livelihood on doctors and] was unable to be cured by anyone, came up behind him and touched the tassel on his cloak. Immediately her bleeding stopped. Jesus then asked, 'Who touched me?' While all were denying it, Peter said, 'Master, the crowds are pushing and pressing in upon you.'

But Jesus said, 'Someone has touched me; for I know that power has gone out from me.' When the

137

woman realized that she had not escaped notice, she came forward trembling. Falling down before him, she explained in the presence of all the people why she had touched him and how she had been healed immediately. He said to her, 'Daughter, your faith has saved you; go in peace.'" (Luke 8:43-48, NAB)

Someone touched me! He knew who and why someone came to touch Him. When you have been touched by your faith, you cannot slink back and be one in the noisy crowd. Jesus calls you forth and you answer Him, although trembling and throwing yourself at His feet in the gaze of everyone, in plain view to proclaim His wondrous miracle in your life.

That woman is me. I've always believed and have had faith and many a time have felt the hand of the Lord on my head – "My daughter go in peace," He said. Then I fall on my knees and say my personal heartfelt praise and give thanks. And then I am one of the crowd.

Not this time. This time, my story is quite like that woman's: I am writing this to everyone who wants to read and listen. I have been asked to come forth from the crowd and witness.

My testimony is a personal narrative of a dire, dreadful ailment, which has taken me on a journey of spiritual discovery. Born and raised a Roman Catholic, I grew up in a conventional household, spent eleven years in Catholic education and thereafter four years at a Catholic college doing graduate studies, later teaching at Catholic schools all my working life and instructing at Sunday school and confirmation classes. You should think that I would be very voluble about proclaiming this faith. No. Not me. True blend-in-the-crowd mentality. Maybe I just took everything good and blessed that came my way as an entitlement, never stopping to think that I should give back, that giving is the other side of the receiving coin. Never stopping to think in my thirties and forties what benevolence is. But now the journey has begun.

I took that first step on this journey on 8 July 2018, when trial and tribulation came down on me like a ton of bricks.

In the two previous months, casual tests were carried out to investigate an abdominal discomfort, and the ultrasound had revealed stones in the gall bladder. Many tiny ones and one big boulder. Phew! That's the relief that comes when medics and technicians decipher the reports and present a diagnosis. Okay, gall stones. No problem. My sister had dealt with those a few years ago, and the surgical procedures to get those stones out were simple. Surgery was scheduled for the not-too-distant months ahead. But a diagnosis does not heal.

So, on that Sunday morning, 8 July 2018, the pain in my abdomen intensified, and I hastened to the emergency wing of the QEII hospital. That day, the rug was pulled from right under my feet. The radiologists examined all those tests results and then handed over a verdict to the doctor I was consulting. She came into the ward very disturbed. "I'm afraid, it's not good news," she said. "They see cancer."

I guess somewhere, sometime, life as you know it, puts its emergency brakes on you. But at that moment, I realized I was not alone. The surreal feeling that the Lord was holding my hand and that He would never let go of it, was real. He hadn't in all my life and wouldn't now.

I was surrounded by family and friends, who propped me up, prayed with and for me and prodded me along. So, the brakes were a wake-up call. Why should this diagnosis turn me inwards and make me focus on myself? There is a whole world out there. There must be another chance for one little benevolent action or one opportunity for me to make a difference in someone's life. Yes, I could look inwards and take a good look in those places that mattered: my heart, my head and my attitude. I was ruminating on these musings.

In the meantime, the blood work and results of the CAT scans came pouring in, introducing previously unknown medical jargon, all pointing to a CA-125 count of 790, placing me on Stage Three of the High Grade Ovarian Cancer ladder.

But the Lord gave me and my husband, Robin, the spiritually-inspired strength to communicate this verdict to our three children, their spouses and our seven grandkids. "You direct the time and our words O Lord." We supplicated to Him before facing the kids on a Whatsapp screen. I didn't think I would have any more pain to come that compared with the pain of this one single act – of spilling out the bad news to the kids. They burst into tears silently, but quickly regained poise. The silence was eerie.

Then came visits to the Cancer Centre and meetings with oncologists, gynecologists, onco-nurses, chemotherapy sessions, blood tests, hospitalization, lung fluid drainage, surgical procedures, and our world as we knew it on its head. But my Lord hadn't done with me yet! He just kept making me stronger in spirit, in energy and kept giving me these wonderful gifts of love and tolerance and patience. I felt guilty that on my part, I only cherished this gifted life from day to ordinary day without recompense.

On September 10, I sailed through that third chemo with flying colours, and weeks later when the blood reports landed on the desk of the oncologist, it was a "eureka" moment. My ovarian cancer cell count (CA-125) fell from 790 to 35. There was euphoria. But was that a catharsis? No. Not yet.

In October, I was called in to undergo a hysterectomy. That was a five-hour surgical procedure with family waiting outside the Operation Room holding their breath and storming heaven. Then when all was done, the Chief surgeon called my husband on the phone and said: "Robin this is great news. It has baffled all of our surgeons. None of us were able to see a trace of cancer." A couple of nurses standing around him watched with joy as he got teary-eyed. Are miracles a myth?

I began to read the psalms daily and reflect on them. The wonderful supplications and the praise and worship that came from these daily readings made me realize all the more from day to wonderful day that the Lord will always stand by my side, quietly, strongly and faithfully.

As this feeling of joy sprang up, so also did the feeling of being an inadequate disciple. Like the woman in the opening lines of this narrative, I couldn't come out in front of the crowd and acknowledge the stream of spiritual fodder that was pouring into my being. I contemplated setting up a blog to share the experience. It didn't happen. Was this a spiritual desert? What could I possibly do that would be more fulfilling to the Lord.

Then came more great news again. I began to witness more healing of the body. By the end of 2018, the CA-125 count dropped from 35 to seven and oncologists were amazed with the speed of recovery.

Then when in that chemotherapy room of the QE II hospital, I rang that bell of hope on New Year's Eve 2018, I was already looking forward to 2019 which saw foreign trips to England in April to celebrate my niece's nuptials, celebrations with family in Toronto, and a long holiday with my daughter and grandsons in New York. 2019 was a great year.

But mortals beware! It's not over till it's over. Upon flying back from New York at the end of 2019, bad tidings hit again. The same cancer, lurking in my lymph nodes, raised that ugly head.

In despair, I turned to Robin and said: "I am sorry, I've disappointed you." As a tear rolled down his cheek, I promised him I would cling to my faith and be strong. So, in faith and trust I tell myself let's move on to another six months of chemo amid a pandemic that was sweeping across the world.

A lot of water has flowed under my life's bridge in the last couple of years. All is well with me now. But what stands out for me most is His hand reaching out to me across the stormy water. That has been my biggest gift. It doesn't matter - the cancer. It is not important - the pain or the uncertainty. It is the gift of faith which is about trust and submission that's all important. Most crucial: It is the joy of recognizing this God-given outpouring of grace and the gift of this ability to accept and surrender to His will. I do not know what – as I journey along – will unfold. Most days I see two sets of footprints in the sands of time, but there are and will be days when I might see one set of prints – these making a deeper impression on the sands - for I know who sits on the shoulder of the Christ making this journey with me.

I have realized that the first thing God did with me was to get me accustomed to rugged reality, so that in time, it's not important what becomes of me, for as long as He will get His way.

I do not want to wither away not having fulfilled the purpose in His plan. If through this journey of a malady, God can bring His plan to fulfillment, then I thank Him for this event in my life.

But I have to leave this account of God's wonderful

presence in my life as an ongoing story. That is because I have yet to see a purpose for myself in God's plan. Maybe I am not made for brilliant moments and the plan is the ordinary – the battles where I fight no one else but myself. Perhaps God has a particular goal for me, and He's leading me there. But could it be that what I call my journey could be God's purpose? He is calling me to depend on Him and His power. I see Him walking on the waves, no shore in sight, just the absolute certainty that all will be well. God's end is to enable me to "see" that He intervenes when there is chaos in my life. I see Him preparing the way for some definite, grand purpose here. Now is actually the process, not the end, which is to glorify Him.

Author's note: In her narrative, Teresa has referred to Robin, her husband, a couple of times. Yes, that Robin is me. She and I have spent forty-seven years in marriage and together have three kids and seven grandkids. She has been a Science and Chemistry teacher for the greater part of her career.

Chapter 9

Dylan Arthur

Fights schizophrenia, suicide callings, before witnessing God's hand in recovery

...the beast of schizophrenia would not loosen its grip on him. Erratically, Dylan would be extremely irate, boisterous and smoke incessantly. One morning, in a fit of temper, unaware of what was going on inside him, he flung a piece of furniture on an image of Jesus Christ in his home, painted by his father, Jossie. That image of Jesus, even today, adorns his home at a L'Arche-affiliated centre in Goa, a southern state of India. "I was in a trance at the time, not aware of what was going on, in the depths of depression, fighting fear and suffering," he says.

Dylan, who is the youngest in a family of seven, grew up in a Catholic home in what was the city of Bombay at the time (now Mumbai) and after graduating from high school, took after his father and got enrolled at the J.J. College of Art in 1988. Five years later, he got his Government Diploma in Art (GDA) and picked up a job in an advertising agency.

It was at this workplace when he first confronted symptoms of schizophrenia. "People at work would look at me strangely, and I would be in a daze not aware of what was going on around me," he says. "I started to feel fear, especially at nights." He says it was at that point, he gradually descended into a dark hole with a string of troubles, first starting out with cigarettes and then alcohol.

"In order to get out of that environment in Mumbai, my brother invited me to Dubai and arranged job interviews for me. It wasn't easy, but I finally managed to sign up a contract with a medium-sized advertising agency. But schizophrenia did not leave my side. It haunted me day and night."

Dylan says he began work in Dubai probably functioning normally for some months. Then the war in the Gulf erupted after Saddam Hussein's invasion of Kuwait. Advertising agencies were the first to be hit as a consequence of a depressed economy.

"At the time, I could see my colleagues at the art studio working against me and then later the studio boss, as well, found fault with me, forcing me to hurl insults at him," Dylan recalls. On one of those days, he says, he struggled to sleep but could not. Then he took an overdose of tranquillizers and woke up late at night the next day. At work the following day, the inevitable followed, and he was fired.

In the next couple of weeks, while without a job in Dubai, depression rolled in and with it waves of loneliness. Dylan hit the bottle on a few occasions until he almost one night descended into a coma. "With alcohol, I would sometimes get irate or lonely. Dubai wasn't working out for me. So, I got on to a flight to Mumbai a week later, almost a year after I had left that city."

The environment around him in Mumbai had transformed. The people he knew had moved on. Struggling with his life, he pursued a job and got one, but lost it in about a week. Apparently, schizophrenic symptoms were intensifying. He says he would hear voices talking to him and see people gazing at him strangely. This job was a non-starter.

Dylan by then was convinced he could not cope with a workplace and so started out on his own and began to present new expressions of the paintings of the great artists at a makeshift studio at home. In those years, he was able to successfully complete works of Judith Leyster, Paulus Potter, Willem Kalf and other masters.

But the beast of schizophrenia would not loosen its grip on him. Erratically, Dylan would be extremely irate and boisterous, smoke incessantly and once in a fit of temper, unaware of what was going on inside him, he flung a piece of furniture on an image of Jesus Christ in his home, painted by his father, Jossie. The image of Jesus, even today, adorns his home at Divya Sadan - a L'Arche-affiliated centre in Goa, a southern state of India. L'Arche is an international institution for people with intellectual disabilities.

"I was in a trance at the time, not aware of what was going on in the depths of my depression, fighting fear and suffering. I loved God, but my faith was not mature then. I would wear several scapulars and patron saint medals as a way of supplicating for my recovery. But my faith was not a sterling one."

"Those were the darkest years of my life: I slipped into bad company and made friends without discerning. As a consequence, I was introduced to blue films and with that lust entered my life. A corrupt friend even tried maliciously to introduce me to drugs. I don't remember succumbing to that pressure. But I do recall an attempted suicide with an overdose of tranquilisers. Apparently, God was watching this drift and intervened. I was hospitalized for a couple of days and discharged. I got a second chance at life."

Not long after that, the family made arrangements for his admission to a hospital that specialized in the care of the intellectually challenged.

"A doctor came home one morning and tranquillized me with an injection. He later escorted me to an ambulance and all I know after that is waking up in a hospital that afternoon, where after the initial treatment, I was given the first of thirteen shock treatments that month. At that point, I began to see God working in my life through my family. That was also the time when I was weaned away from cigarettes and alcohol. That was the biggest miracle in my life."

Dylan was then transferred to a rehabilitation centre in the state of Goa, where he spent eight months before being discharged. His arrival at the new home in Goa and his meeting with his mother after some nine months was a heart-breaking moment.

Mother, who was diagnosed with Alzheimer's at the time of his admission to the mental care hospital in Mumbai, was now in an advanced stage of that disease. "That, in fact, sobered me down," he says.

"Of course, there were security fears about a future without mom. But soon after being discharged from the rehab centre, I was enrolled at Cooj, a day care therapy centre, and the recovery process began there. I found God through my family when in 2010, after my mom's passing away, I began independent living at a hostel."

A few years later, while still working on therapy at Cooj, Dylan quit the hostel and took up residence at Divya Sadan and that was where life began to change for him. Dylan became prolific with his work as an artist and was interviewed by the local Press. Some of his work has been published in a German magazine. His charcoal paintings commissioned by a pastor, adorn the walls of a church in Goa. He has spoken at various events delivering a testimony of his life which has swung from the trials of schizophrenia to the witness of a new, changed life and now YouTube carries a video interview of his troubled past but also testifies to how God extricated him from it.

"Since 2012 I have seen that prayer changes things. I rely on my mother's prayers, and I know God is working in my life."

Author's note: Dylan is my brother and the youngest in a family of seven. His battle with schizophrenia is something all of us have witnessed with great pain and his recovery with gratifying joy.

Chapter 10

Lorna Wade

He kept repeating in despair:
"Nobody informed us she is dying."

When my eyes gradually began to focus, I saw a priest praying over me and crossing my forehead with holy oil and it began to dawn on me that I was being administered the last rites. I believe I began to feel strengthened physically and spiritually after that.

It was sometime in February 1971 that I began to run a persistent high fever, and all of the antibiotics I ingested in fifteen days - prescribed by my family doctor - resulted in no remission whatsoever. It was then that I was advised to see a specialist at the Holy Spirit Hospital in Mumbai, and I was admitted for investigations. I was very comfortable with the administration of this hospital, having experienced the quality of care by their nuns and nurses there, when a year previous I delivered my daughter Vimla at that hospital.

They gave me a four-bed room, one of which was shared by another endearing nun from the missionaries of Charity. I spent an interesting week there with Sr. Priscilla, chatting, singing hymns and praying together before going to bed. She was admitted for recurring low range fever without a prognosis.

As for me, after enduring two weeks of high temperatures brought down with medication and ice packs, the nuns decided to move me to a private room for priority care. They provided a bed for my husband Tony, sympathetic of the fact that he spent the nights there, leaving the hospital in the morning to get to work.

What followed was a series of tests: blood was drawn twice or thrice a day and administering those medications intravenously was a challenging job for the nurses who had to probe my veins which by then were collapsing. So, they would look for them in my legs.

Sternum puncture, lumber puncture, cauterisations, all kinds of tests were conducted to no avail and a diagnosis could not be arrived at. Then came the barium meal test to which my body strongly reacted - my pulse was failing me, and for moments a veil of darkness would enshroud me.

One morning, I woke up with medical hardware all around me. I was wrapped up in wires and tubes that were connected to monitors and some of those tubes were lodged in my nostrils. At a critical moment, I saw a sea of blurred faces and heard a faint voice that I reckoned was that of my father-in law. He kept repeating in distress: "Nobody informed us she is dying. Nobody informed us she is dying."

When my eyes gradually began to focus, I saw a priest praying over me and signing the cross on my forehead with holy oil. It began to dawn on me, then, that I was being administered the last rites. I believe, I began to feel strengthened spiritually after that.

Nonetheless, the fever continued to race on, at one point spiralling to 107 degrees Fahrenheit. I heard the doctor fearfully whisper those numbers to the nurse beside him. Soon after, my physician finally referred me to an eminent medical specialist, who came in to see me for ten minutes, wrote out a prescription for high doses of Penicillin to be administered intravenously and walked out of the room leaving behind a whopping invoice for medical consultation rendered.

By now, I was wasting away rapidly: my weight had dropped to twenty-five kilos, and a fine layer of skin clung to my bones. The unkindest cut of all, however, was that in those desperate moments, my heart was aching with deep longings to cradle my little baby Vimla in my arms. And that was what I could not do. Barely a month ago, then, we had celebrated her first birthday and now the urge to cuddle her and rock her to sleep was a burning one. It was agonizing for me to watch her from my bed and fight the temptation to reach out and grab her.

Amidst all of this anguish, I was struggling with a new trauma driven by hallucinations of hideous and repulsive demons taunting me at my bedside. I would visually dig a hole in the ground and bury them as deeply as I could, but they would surface again and torment me. I recall putting huge boulders over them, but the agony did not abate. The struggle was fierce.

It was in this state of turmoil that the door of my room, one day, barely opened, and I was delighted to see not a white-coat medic make an entry, but a priest with a smooth bald pate that almost shone a light - in a metaphorical sense - and before he could withdraw his partially visible cassocked frame, I called out to him: "Father, I'd like to speak to you." He responded. "I'll be back."

He came to my room almost two hours later. But that was the start of something great. This priest, Fr. Sopena, subsequently came to see me at all times of day

to sit by my bedside for the next ten weeks that followed. At one time, I heard loud voices in the corridor
at about 11 o'clock in the night, and it turned out that
Sr. Willibraud, the assistant Administrator at the time,
was, in a light-hearted way, chiding Fr. Sopena for
coming to see a patient at a restricted time.

That day, he had gone to the neighbouring city of
Pune for a day's spiritual retreat, but that did not deter
him from visiting me the same night to say the daily
prayer that he and Tony would say on bended knee
every night in supplication to the Lord.

On one of those days, I remember he chose to pick
a Missal (a liturgical book) to lead them into prayer.
But turning its pages that evening, he stopped abruptly
at a point seeming somewhat agitated. He thumped the
Missal on my bed saying with some delightful Spanish
fury: "That cannot be: 'Jesus suffered, and He was a
sinless man.' We never suffer for our sins."

That utterance made by my bedside that evening
was one of those first gospel truths that enlightened me
and led me to perceive God in a new light. But, of
course, there were more to come from dear Fr. Sopena
in the many years of our friendship. He never ever
offered me advice. I learnt from example.

Fr. Sopena continued to be my dearest friend for

the next forty years until the time when he passed away in 2016. It was no coincidence that my family and I were in Mumbai when he was ready to bid farewell to the multitude of people to whom he reflected His loving Saviour Jesus. I felt so blessed to be by his side. He was the epitome of Jesus' love. He was an assigned angel that God sent to me as an expression of His abounding love for me and through which lens I saw this love around me in my family and my friends who were by my side during this time of tribulation.

Even as I was slowly wasting away, the fever raged on. *Prayers of Life* by Michel Quoist, a book my brother Ivan gave me, took me through those days of uncertainty and got me to realize that Jesus was the only reality in my life and that He was in control. His love was so abounding. It was made manifest in my family and among those who took care of me: the doctors, nurses, nuns and those who visited me. I was never alone and never felt miserable. The scriptural assurance in Deuteronomy 31:8 (NAB), "It is the LORD who goes before you; he will be with you and will never fail you or forsake you. So do not fear or be dismayed" comes to mind now. And again, "With age-old love I have loved you; so I have kept my mercy toward you." (Jeremiah 31:3, NAB).

Those were days, I remember with gratitude to a

God I can never thank enough and who loves us unconditionally. He took me through the storm holding onto me with His love. "He will sit refining and purifying silver" (Malachi 3:3, NAB). I believe, that like the silversmith, who holds onto his metal in the fire and takes it out only when he sees his image in it, so does our loving God never abandon or forsake us when we go through the fires of life. He holds onto us all the time and pulls us out only when we are thoroughly cleansed of all the dross that sticks to us, when we are refined, purified and He can see His image in us. What a loving God we serve.

Then the miracle of my life all at once manifested itself at dawn one day. The dark clouds receded, the hideous demons were crushed, the spiralling fever crumbled and evanesced. I did the disappearing trick and left my room in a wheelchair and headed for the end of the corridor to commiserate with another patient on a dying bed.

The embattled doctors and nurses were struck with fear when they realized I was not in my room. The great hunt for Lorna on a death bed had begun with doctors and nurses scrambling across the corridors of the hospital looking for me. But that was some brief anguish. The nurses were visibly disturbed when they finally saw me, but quickly did a fever check and were stunned to see that the stubborn, nagging fever of a couple of months had vanished into thin air, overnight.

The neurologist, Dr. Manikal, was pleasantly surprised, too, but told the nurses not to dampen my spirit. "This woman has a high morale. She's healed," he said. He was suggesting that I should feel free to move about and be social. It was a surreal resurrection.

That was the 30th of May 1971. It was the feast of the Holy Spirit. My fever left me in a way that you would drop a hot potato. What a perfect day to recall forever and to bring me to the realisation of the Holy Spirit in my life.

The nuns at the Holy Spirit Hospital were stupefied at the miracle that baffled everybody. So, they invited doctors, nurses, family members and friends to a Mass celebrated by Fr. Sopena and then to a fellowship to share a testimony of God's infinite love in the miracle He had wrought for me and my family.

There was great jubilation at the party that followed Mass. I was presented with an antique statuette of Christ, one that is my most prized treasure to this day. Sr. Carmelann insisted that she take me home personally, saying: "It's an honor to take home one who is Resurrected." I will always cherish the love and care they nurtured me with. They sent me little inspirational notes in my meal trays and took special care to plate up with nourishing food to pull me out of that atrophied state.

What a revelation for me! I was aware of God as my Heavenly Father and Jesus His son in the flesh at all times. But in this crisis of my life, He introduced Himself to me in the Holy Spirit who lives and reigns in me, Whom He has given to all of us to lead us, guard us and guide us on the path that leads to Eternal Life.

Psalm 30 speaks to me of God's love that pulled me out of the grave to give me a more meaningful life with Him on this journey. I must share this with you:

> *I will exalt you,* LORD, *for you lifted me out of the depths and did not let my enemies gloat over me.*
> LORD *my God, I called to you for help and you healed me.*
> *You,* LORD, *brought me up from the realm of the dead; you spared me from going down to the pit.*
> *Sing the praises of the* LORD, *you his faithful people; praise his holy name.*
> *For his anger lasts only a moment, but his favor lasts a lifetime; weeping may stay for the night, but rejoicing comes in the morning.*
> *When I felt secure, I said, "I will never be shaken."*

LORD, *when you favored me, you made my royal mountain stand firm; but when you hid your face, I was dismayed.*

To you, LORD, I called; to the Lord I cried for mercy: "What is gained if I am silenced, if I go down to the pit?

Will the dust praise you? Will it proclaim your faithfulness?

Hear, LORD, and be merciful to me; LORD, be my help."

You turned my wailing into dancing; you removed my sackcloth and clothed me with joy,

That my heart may sing your praises and not be silent. LORD my God, I will praise you forever.

Author's Note: Lorna is my elder sister. I watched her fighting for life on a hospital bed with great sadness, as I sat beside her for those many nights, revising my literature essays and preparing for the final year Bachelor of Arts papers I would write in the morning. Lorna, who began a career in teaching, finally ended it as a senior banker.

EPILOGUE

I do not know if this book has been able to prick the ear and rivet the mind of ardent seekers of the truth, although that is what I fervently hope has occurred. I have, however, tried to share my own thoughts with you, many of them shaping themselves over time from the experience of the mystery of life. I have also shared those mystical stories of great minds that speak about a life transformation.

Faith cannot be grasped like you would grasp a theorem. It comes to you as you view the conundrums of life from the vantage point of a third eye – the one from the heart. It's that spiritual strength within us that Jesus summons to heal the leper, the blind, the crippled and to resurrect the dead.

In this book, I have tried to share the experience of so many who have looked squarely at suffering and death in the face and stood up to it, content in the pro-mise of eternal salvation which the death and resurrec-tion of Jesus brings to all who repent and come to him. Unfortunately, while many revel in the thought of going to heaven, no one wants to die in order to get there.

The testimonies presented in this book are real life confessions of prominent and ordinary people who have either felt the healing or saving hand of God in a near-death experience or in other ways. I hope these stories have touched and inspired you and driven into you a new sense of hope that when dark clouds enshroud you, your faith will heal you.

If *Experiencing God* can draw you to that Faith Store, that Upper Room where you might be able to, like the apostle Thomas, put your finger in His side proclaiming, "My Lord and my God," then that's a moment of great celebration because there will be rejoicing in heaven...

ACKNOWLEDGEMENTS

This book, I think, is an important sequel to my previous book *Science and the God Elusion* because it now seeks to transport the reader to a new threshold of discernment having bridged the gaps in understanding of how the universe was born and how life evolved. *Experiencing God – Thoughts and Testimonies* addresses those great conundrums-of-life questions that niggle the seeker of the truth, the wilderness wanderer and the agnostic.

As well, with this book, I did also want to bring a new conversation to the table pointing to the fact that the search for the 'God mystery' cannot be pursued by an intellectual tool - such as science is - in worlds where fact and truth are established by empirical evidence alone. That pursuit would, forever, be futile because science would be looking for God in the wrong place.

So, now that the book is here, I have a great deal to be grateful for. There have been many involved in bringing this book to fruition and therefore many to whom I must acknowledge gratitude. Firstly, I thank my publisher Dr. Sebastian Mahfood, OP, of En Route Books and Media for taking up my proposed book *Experiencing God - Thoughts and Testimonies* for publication. It has been a great pleasure to work with him. I must also thank Dr. Kevin Vost for introducing me to Dr. Mahfood.

I acknowledge with gratitude the many publishing houses, universities, scientific journals and research organizations that graciously granted me permissions to reprint quotes from their copyrighted material under the fair use provisions of the copyright law.

I am also indebted to the several individuals and organization trustees who have either contributed testimonies to this book or granted me permission to tell their stories. I am grateful to *Postmedia* for excerpts taken from its special report *2000 years of Christianity* and which have been reprinted in Saint Paul's conversion story in my book; C.S. Lewis Pte Ltd for permission to reprint the C.S. Lewis conversion story with excerpts taken from Lewis's book *Mere Christianity*; Biologos for the permission to reproduce excerpts from Dr. Francis Collins' presentation at the 2019 BioLogos Conference; Joseph Pearce and Kevin Vost, for their gracious submission of their testimonies; *The Abolition Project* for the permission to reprint the story of John Newton and to Dylan Arthur, Lorna Wade and my wife, Teresa, who graciously submitted their new-life testimonies.

I am immensely grateful to Rev. Fr. Owen Connolly, a priest in the Archdiocese of Halifax/Dartmouth, who gleaned through the book in order to write the back cover blurb. Fr. Connolly's wisdom has been influential in the writing of at least one chapter of this book.

I am grateful to Ivan Arthur who graciously accepted my invitation to present the Foreword. Among the many books he has authored is *The Fourteen Stations* – the official souvenir of Pope John Paul II's visit to India in 1986.

I must also acknowledge my gratitude to Stephen Cunningham, who patiently, but with an eagle's eye, has gleaned through this book, and made editorial recommendations.

Finally, this book would not have been possible without the influential advice presented by my dear wife, Teresa, and the patient discourses I have had with her in the course of writing this book. I have always been grateful to her.

REFERENCES

Section 1

Chapter 1

1. Thomas Merton, *Seven Storey Mountain* (Boston: Houghton Mifflin Harcourt, 1998), p. 123. Reprinted with permission.
2. Mike McHargue, *Finding God in the Waves: How I Lost My Faith and Found It Again Through Science* (New York City: Convergent Books/Penguin Random House, 2016), p.128. Reprinted with permission.
3. Kurt Vonnegut, *A Man Without a Country* (Seven Stories Press), p. 66. Reprinted with permission.
4. Jeffrey Lidke, "Interpreting across Mystical Boundaries: An analysis of Samadhi in the Trika Kaula Tradition." *Theory and Practice of Yoga: Essays in honour of Gerald James Larson* (Boston: Brill, 2005), pp. 143-180.
5. J. McClenon, "Wondrous Events," *Encyclopedia of Religion and Society* (Philadelphia: University of Penn-

sylvania Press, 1994).

6. James R. Horne, *Mysticism and Vocation* (Waterloo, ON: Wilfred Laurier University Press, 1996).

7. Jerome Gellman, "Mysticism." *The Stanford Encyclopedia of Philosophy* (Summer 2011 edition). Online at https://plato.stanford.edu/entries/mysticism/

8. John Cornwell, *Darwin's Angel: An Angelic Riposte to The God Delusion* (London: Profile Books Ltd., 2009), p. 44. Reprinted with permission.

9. Russell Goodman, "William James," *Stanford Encyclopedia of Philosophy Archive.* Online at https://plato.stanford.edu/archives/spr2019/entries/james/ Reprinted with permission.

10. "Mysticism," *Wikipedia* https://en.wikipedia.org/wiki/Mysticism

11. Ibid.

12. Peter Bernard Clarke, *New Religions in Global Perspective: A Study of Religious Change in the Modern World* (New York: Routledge, 2005), p. 209.

13. "Mysticism," *Wikipedia* https://en.wikipedia.org/wiki/Mysticism

14. Ahmed Zarruq, Zaineb Istrabadi, Hamza Yusuf Hanson *The Principles of Sufism* (Chicago: Amal Press, 2008).

Chapter 2

1. Mike McHargue, *Finding God in the Waves: How I Lost My Faith and Found It Again Through Science* (New York City: Convergent Books/Penguin Random House, 2016), p.156. Reprinted with permission.
2. Richard Dawkins, *The God Delusion* (Boston: Houghton Mifflin Harcourt, 2006), p. 125. Reprinted with permission.
3. C. Andrade and R. Radhakrishnan, "The Biochemistry of Belief," *Indian Journal of Psychiatry* 51, no. 4 (Oct-Dec, 2009): 247-253.
4. V.A. Barnes, H.C. Davis, J.B. Murzynowski, and F.A. Treiber, "Impact of meditation on resting and ambulatory blood pressure and heart rate in youth." *Psychosom Med.* 66, no. 6 (Nov-Dec, 2004): 909-14.
5. E.E. Solberg, O Ekeberg, A. Holen, F. Ingjer, L Sandvik, P.A. Standal, A. Vikman, "Hemodynamic changes during long meditation." *Applied Psychophysiology Biofeedback* 29, no. 3 (Sept. 2004):213-21.
6. D. Cysarz, and A. Büssing, "Cardiorespiratory synchronization during Zen meditation." *European Journal of Applied Physiology* 95, no. 1 (June 7, 2005): 88-95.

7. E.E. Solberg, A. Holen, Ø. Ekeberg, B. Østerud, R. Halvorsen, and L. Sandvik, "The effects of long meditation on plasma melatonin and blood serotonin." *Med Sci Monit.* 10, no. 3 (March 2004): 96-101.

8. R.J. Davidson, J. Kabat-Zinn, J. Schumacher, M. Rosenkranz, D. Muller, S.F. Santorelli, F. Urbanowski, A. Harrington, K. Bonus, and J.F. Sheridan, "Alterations in brain and immune function produced by mindfulness meditation." *Psychosom Med.* 65, no. 4 (Jul-Aug 2003): 564-70.

9. R. Bonadonna, "Meditation's impact on chronic illness." *Holist Nurs Pract.* 17, no. 6 (Nov-Dec. 2003): 309-19.

10. American Cancer Society: https://en.wikipedia.org/wiki/Faith_healing

11. Helen Dukas and Banesh Hoffman. *Albert Einstein: The Human Side - New Glimpses From His Archives (1979),* (Princeton: Princeton University Press, 1981), p. 66.

12. Claudia Kalb, "Can religion improve health? While the debate rages in journals and med schools, more Americans ask for doctors' prayers". *Newsweek.* Archived from the original on 2004-02-03.

Chapter 3

1. "Black Death," *Wikipedia*. https://en.wikipedia.org/wiki/Black-Death

2. "Spanish Flu," *Wikipedia*. https://en.wikipedia.org/wiki/Spanish_flu

3. "World War II Casualties," *Wikipedia*. https://en.wikipedia.org/wiki/World_War_II_casualties

4. Gavin Matthews and Gareth Black, "Pain and Pandemics: Does A Good God Exist?" *YouTube*. https://youtu.be/U2MBap0GTUc

5., Charles Darwin, *On the Origin of Species,* The Project Gutenberg eBook, Chapter III, Struggle for Existence, 11th paragraph. Reprinted with permission.

6. Extract from a presentation by Royal Pandit Bhikkhu Saranapala at the first Spiritual Diversity Conference hosted in 2011 in Halifax.

7. "Islamic View of Death," *Wikipedia*. https://en.wikipedia.org/wiki/Islamic_view_of_death; Buturovic, Amila (2016). *Carved in Stone, Etched in Memory*. Routledge. p. 34. *Maariful Quran* by Muhammad Shafi Usmani. English translation by Maulana Ahmed Khalil Aziz. Vol 8; p. 534. (Sura 67, verse 2). Karachi.

Chapter 4

1. "Where do we come from? What are We? Where are we going?" en.wikipedia.org/wiki/Where_Do_We_Come_From%3F_What_Are_We%3F_Where_Are_We_Going%3F

2. "*Origin* by Dan Brown," *Wikipedia*, https://en.wikipedia.org/wiki/Origin_(Brown_novel)

3. Francis Collins, in an address at the opening of the BioLogos conference in 2019. Reprinted with permission.

4. L. Gerald Schroeder, *The Hidden Face of God* (New York: Simon & Schuster, 2002), p.58. Reprinted with permission.

5. Charles Darwin, *On the Origin of Species*, The Project Gutenberg eBook, Chapter X1V: Recapitulation and Conclusion, 39th paragraph. Reprinted with permission.

6. Billy Graham, *The Billy Graham Literary Trust*. Reprinted with permission. All rights reserved, 2001.

7. Francis Collins, in an address at the opening of the BioLogos conference in 2019. Reprinted with permission.

Chapter 5

1. "Sin," *Wikipedia*. https://en.wikipedia.org/wiki/Sin

2. "Pelagius," *Wikipedia*. https://en.wikipedia.org/wiki/Pelagius

3. Ibid.

4. "Jewish Views on Sin," *Wikipedia*. https://en.wikipedia.org/wiki/Jewish_views_on_sin.

5. "Bahá'i Views on Sin," *Wikipedia*. https://en.wikipedia.org/wiki/Bahá'i_views_on_sin

6. "Religious and Philosophical View of Albert Einstein," *Wikipedia*. https://en.wikipedia.org/wiki/Religious_and_philosophical_views_of_Albert_Einstein, Martin Gardner, *The Night Is Large: Collected Essays, 1938-1995*. (New York: St. Martin's Griffin, 1997). p. 430.

7. A. Pabl Iannone, "Determinism." *Dictionary of World Philosophy*. (New York: Taylor & Francis, 2001), p. 194.

8. Wentzel Van Huyssteen, "Theological Determinism," *Encyclopedia of Science and Religion* (2003). Macmillan Reference, p. 217.

9. Ibid. See Martin Luther and Desiderius Erasmus.

10. *Catechism of the Roman Catholic Church*, section 600.

11. Syed Moustaffa Al Qazwini, *Discovering Islam* (Costa

Mesa: CA, Islamic Educational Center of Orange County, 2001). Reprinted with permission.

12. Edward N. Zalta (ed.), "Determinism and Alternative Possibilities." *The Stanford Encyclopedia of Philosophy* (Summer 2020 Edition), https://plato.stanford.edu/archives/sum2020/entries/compatibilism Reprinted with permission.

13. Daniel Defoe, *The Life and Adventures of Robinson Crusoe* (1919). Project Gutenberg eBook, Chapter XV, paragraph 14.

Chapter 6

1. Joint statement by ILO, FAO, IFAD and WHO. 13 October 2020.

2. Most Americans Say Coronavirus Outbreak Has Impacted their Lives, Pew Research Center, Washington, DC, March 30, 2020. www.pewresearch.org/social-trends/2020/03/30/most-americans-say-coronavirus-outbreak-has-impacted-their-lives/

3. Stephen Hawking, *A Brief History of Time* (New York: Bantam/Penguin Random House, 1998), p. 133-135. Reprinted with permission.

4. John Cornwell, *Darwin's Angel: An Angelic Riposte to*

The God Delusion (London: Profile Books Ltd., 2009), p. 64. Reprinted with permission.

5. "Mother Teresa," *Wikipedia.* https://en.wikipedia.org/ wiki/Mother_Teresa

6. T'RUAH: The Rabbinic Call for Human Rights. Online at http://www.truah.org/wp-content/uploads/2018/12/ TRUAH-2016-2017-Annual-Report.pdf. Reprinted with permission.

7. AKDN. https://www.akdn.org/about-us/frequently-asked-questions. Reprinted with permission.

Section 2

Paul's conversion to Christianity

1. "2000 years of Christianity, a special report of the *National Post*," p.8, Courtesy: Postmedia. Reprinted with permission.

2. Ibid, p.4/p.5.

3. Ibid, p. 22/p.41.

C.S. Lewis

1. C. S. Lewis, *Surprised by Joy: The Shape of My Early Life.* (London: Harvest Books, 1966). https://en.wikipedia.

org/ wiki/C._S._Lewis

2. "The Golden Key: Home to the George McDonald Society." http://www.george-macdonald.com/resources1/page/ cs_lewis.html

3. C.S. Lewis, *MERE CHRISTIANITY © copyright CS Lewis Pte Ltd 1942, 1943, 1944, 1952.* Reprinted with permission.

4. Excerpt from a presentation by Dr. Francis Collins at the opening of the 2019 BioLogos Conference. Reprinted with permission.

5. C.S. Lewis, MERE CHRISTIANITY © *copyright* CS Lewis Pte Ltd 1942, 1943, 1944, 1952. Reprinted with permission.

6. Ibid.

Dr. Francis Collins

This story was written by the author using extracts taken from a presentation by Dr. Francis Collins at the 2019 Biologos Conference. The story is reprinted with permission.

Horatio Gates Spafford

1. Horatio Spafford, Anna Spafford, *Family Tragedy – The American Colony in Jerusalem.* Library of Congress. https://www.loc.gov/exhibits/americancolony/amcolony-family.html
2. Horatio Spafford, Anna Spafford. *Family Tragedy – The American Colony in Jerusalem.* Library of Congress. https://www.loc.gov/exhibits/americancolony/images/ac0006s.jpg
3. Sandy Hancock, *Letting Go: Pathway to an Amazing Life.* (Bloomington, IN: iUniverse, 2008), p. 11.
4. "Horatio Spafford," *Wikipedia.* https://en.wikipedia.org/wiki/Horatio_Spafford

John Newton

This story was provided courtesy of *The Abolition Project* abolition.e2bn.org/people_35.html

www.ingramcontent.com/pod-product-compliance
Lightning Source LLC
Chambersburg PA
CBHW052001090426
42741CB00008B/1495